■SCHOL Apr. 2013

# MAY WITHDRAWN
# Monthly Idea Book

## Ready-to-Use Templates, Activities, Management Tools, and More—for Every Day of the Month

## Karen Sevaly

SO-AEI-619

New York • Toronto • London • Auckland • Sydney **Teaching**
Mexico City • New Delhi • Hong Kong • Buenos Aires *Resources*

## DEDICATION

*This book is dedicated to teachers and children everywhere.*

Cover design by Maria Lilja
Cover art by Jillian Phillips
Interior design by Melinda Belter
Illustrations by Karen Sevaly with additional artwork by Sue Dennen and Patrick Girouard

ISBN 978-0-545-37941-0

1 2 3 4 5 6 7 8 9 10    40    19 18 17 16 15 14 13

# CONTENTS

**INTRODUCTION** . . . . . . . . . . . . . . . . . . . . . . . . . . . . . . . . . . . . . . . . . 8

What's Inside . . . . . . . . . . . . . . . . . . . . . . . . . . . . . . . . . . . . . . 9

How to Use This Book . . . . . . . . . . . . . . . . . . . . . . . . . . . . . . 11

Meeting the Standards . . . . . . . . . . . . . . . . . . . . . . . . . . . . . 16

**CALENDAR TIME**

Getting Started . . . . . . . . . . . . . . . . . . . . . . . . . . . . . . . . . . . 17

**Reproducible Patterns**

Calendar . . . . . . . . . . . . . . . . . . . . . . . . . . . . . . . . . . . . . . . . 19

Celebrations This Month . . . . . . . . . . . . . . . . . . . . . . . . . . . . 20

Calendar Header . . . . . . . . . . . . . . . . . . . . . . . . . . . . . . . . . . 24

What's the Weather? Body Template . . . . . . . . . . . . . . . . . . . 25

## FAVORITE TOPICS

**PLANTS AND FLOWERS**

Introduction and Suggested Activities . . . . . . . . . . . . . . . . . 27

**Reproducible Patterns**

Flower Word Find . . . . . . . . . . . . . . . . . . . . . . . . . . . . . . . . . 30

Parts-of-a-Flower Diagram . . . . . . . . . . . . . . . . . . . . . . . . . . 31

My Gardening Report . . . . . . . . . . . . . . . . . . . . . . . . . . . . . . 32

Matching Flowers and Pots . . . . . . . . . . . . . . . . . . . . . . . . . . 37

Skills Practice Page . . . . . . . . . . . . . . . . . . . . . . . . . . . . . . . 38

Blooming Flower . . . . . . . . . . . . . . . . . . . . . . . . . . . . . . . . . . 39

Flower Greeting Cards . . . . . . . . . . . . . . . . . . . . . . . . . . . . . 40

## MEXICO

Introduction and Suggested Activities . . . . . . . . . . . . . . . . . . . . . . . . . . . 43

**Reproducible Patterns**

Spanish Word Find . . . . . . . . . . . . . . . . . . . . . . . . . . . . . . . . . . . . . . . 46

Mexican Dancers . . . . . . . . . . . . . . . . . . . . . . . . . . . . . . . . . . . . . . . . 47

Flag of Mexico . . . . . . . . . . . . . . . . . . . . . . . . . . . . . . . . . . . . . . . . . . 48

South-of-the-Border Stationery . . . . . . . . . . . . . . . . . . . . . . . . . . . . . . 49

Maya Pyramid Staircase . . . . . . . . . . . . . . . . . . . . . . . . . . . . . . . . . . . 50

Aztec Calendar Stone . . . . . . . . . . . . . . . . . . . . . . . . . . . . . . . . . . . . . 51

Spanish Bingo Word Cards . . . . . . . . . . . . . . . . . . . . . . . . . . . . . . . . . 52

Spanish Bingo Game Board . . . . . . . . . . . . . . . . . . . . . . . . . . . . . . . . . 53

Fiesta Finger Puppets . . . . . . . . . . . . . . . . . . . . . . . . . . . . . . . . . . . . . 54

## MOTHER'S DAY

Introduction and Suggested Activities . . . . . . . . . . . . . . . . . . . . . . . . . . . 55

**Reproducible Patterns**

Family Word Find . . . . . . . . . . . . . . . . . . . . . . . . . . . . . . . . . . . . . . . . 59

Mother's Day Tea-Party Invitations . . . . . . . . . . . . . . . . . . . . . . . . . . . . 60

Just-for-You Mini-Book . . . . . . . . . . . . . . . . . . . . . . . . . . . . . . . . . . . . 61

Doorknob Bouquet Basket . . . . . . . . . . . . . . . . . . . . . . . . . . . . . . . . . . 63

Paper-Flower Pledges . . . . . . . . . . . . . . . . . . . . . . . . . . . . . . . . . . . . . 64

3-D Daisy Greeting Card . . . . . . . . . . . . . . . . . . . . . . . . . . . . . . . . . . . 65

Roses-Are-Red Greeting Card . . . . . . . . . . . . . . . . . . . . . . . . . . . . . . . 66

## BIRDS

Introduction and Suggested Activities . . . . . . . . . . . . . . . . . . . . . . . . . . . . 67

**Reproducible Patterns**

Bird Word Find . . . . . . . . . . . . . . . . . . . . . . . . . . . . . . . . . . . . . . . 72

Bird Diagram . . . . . . . . . . . . . . . . . . . . . . . . . . . . . . . . . . . . . . . . 73

My Bird Watching Book . . . . . . . . . . . . . . . . . . . . . . . . . . . . . . . . . 74

Bird-Watching Visor . . . . . . . . . . . . . . . . . . . . . . . . . . . . . . . . . . . 82

Bird Sequencing Cards . . . . . . . . . . . . . . . . . . . . . . . . . . . . . . . . . 83

Bird's Nest Board Game . . . . . . . . . . . . . . . . . . . . . . . . . . . . . . . . . 84

Bird Bingo Game Board . . . . . . . . . . . . . . . . . . . . . . . . . . . . . . . . . 86

Repeat Bird Patterns . . . . . . . . . . . . . . . . . . . . . . . . . . . . . . . . . . . 87

Flying Birds Mobile . . . . . . . . . . . . . . . . . . . . . . . . . . . . . . . . . . . . 88

Birdhouse Picture Props . . . . . . . . . . . . . . . . . . . . . . . . . . . . . . . . . 89

Duck Page Framer . . . . . . . . . . . . . . . . . . . . . . . . . . . . . . . . . . . . . 90

Feathered-Friends Reading Log . . . . . . . . . . . . . . . . . . . . . . . . . . . . 91

## ANIMALS OF AFRICA

Introduction and Suggested Activities . . . . . . . . . . . . . . . . . . . . . . . . . . . . 92

**Reproducible Patterns**

Animals-of-Africa Word Find . . . . . . . . . . . . . . . . . . . . . . . . . . . . . . 97

Send-Home Field Trip Form . . . . . . . . . . . . . . . . . . . . . . . . . . . . . . . 98

Field Trip Mini-Book . . . . . . . . . . . . . . . . . . . . . . . . . . . . . . . . . . . 99

## CONTENTS

Animal Report . . . . . . . . . . . . . . . . . . . . . . . . . . . . . . . . . . . . . . . . . . . . 101

Stand-Up Animals . . . . . . . . . . . . . . . . . . . . . . . . . . . . . . . . . . . . . . . . . 102

Lion Puppet . . . . . . . . . . . . . . . . . . . . . . . . . . . . . . . . . . . . . . . . . . . . . . 108

Hippo Puppet . . . . . . . . . . . . . . . . . . . . . . . . . . . . . . . . . . . . . . . . . . . . . 109

Elephant Puppet . . . . . . . . . . . . . . . . . . . . . . . . . . . . . . . . . . . . . . . . . . .110

Monkey-Tail Note . . . . . . . . . . . . . . . . . . . . . . . . . . . . . . . . . . . . . . . . . 112

Lion Page Framer . . . . . . . . . . . . . . . . . . . . . . . . . . . . . . . . . . . . . . . . . 113

Hippo Picture Prop . . . . . . . . . . . . . . . . . . . . . . . . . . . . . . . . . . . . . . . . 115

Giraffe Picture Prop . . . . . . . . . . . . . . . . . . . . . . . . . . . . . . . . . . . . . . . . 116

Amazing African Animals Book Cover . . . . . . . . . . . . . . . . . . . . . . . . . . 117

## CIRCUS

Introduction and Suggested Activities. . . . . . . . . . . . . . . . . . . . . . . . . . . 118

### Reproducible Patterns

Circus Word Find . . . . . . . . . . . . . . . . . . . . . . . . . . . . . . . . . . . . . . . . . 123

Clown Skills Wheel. . . . . . . . . . . . . . . . . . . . . . . . . . . . . . . . . . . . . . . . 124

Clown Face. . . . . . . . . . . . . . . . . . . . . . . . . . . . . . . . . . . . . . . . . . . . . . . 126

Clown Picture Prop . . . . . . . . . . . . . . . . . . . . . . . . . . . . . . . . . . . . . . . . 128

Elephant Picture Prop . . . . . . . . . . . . . . . . . . . . . . . . . . . . . . . . . . . . . . 129

Movable Clown Puppet . . . . . . . . . . . . . . . . . . . . . . . . . . . . . . . . . . . . . 130

Big-Top Finger Puppets . . . . . . . . . . . . . . . . . . . . . . . . . . . . . . . . . . . . . 132

Clown Page Framer . . . . . . . . . . . . . . . . . . . . . . . . . . . . . . . . . . . . . . . . 134

Elephant Book Cover. . . . . . . . . . . . . . . . . . . . . . . . . . . . . . . . . . . . . . . 135

## AWARDS, INCENTIVES, AND MORE

Getting Started . . . . . . . . . . . . . . . . . . . . . . . . . . . . . . . . . . . . . . . . 136

### Reproducible Patterns

Bookmarks . . . . . . . . . . . . . . . . . . . . . . . . . . . . . . . . . . . . . . . . . . . 138

Pencil Toppers . . . . . . . . . . . . . . . . . . . . . . . . . . . . . . . . . . . . . . . . 139

Send-Home Notes . . . . . . . . . . . . . . . . . . . . . . . . . . . . . . . . . . . . . 140

Student of the Week Certificate . . . . . . . . . . . . . . . . . . . . . . . . . . . . 141

Certificate of Recognition. . . . . . . . . . . . . . . . . . . . . . . . . . . . . . . . . 142

## ANSWER KEY . . . . . . . . . . . . . . . . . . . . . . . . . . . . . . . . . . . . . . . . 143

# INTRODUCTION

Welcome to the original Monthly Idea Book series! This book was written especially for teachers getting ready to teach topics related to the month of May.

Each book in this month-by-month series is filled with dozens of ideas for PreK–3 classrooms. Activities connect to the Common Core State Standards for Reading (Foundational Skills), among other subjects, to help you meet the needs of your students. (For more information, see page 16.)

Most everything you need to prepare the lessons and activities in this resource is included, such as:

- calendar and weather-related props

- book cover patterns and stationery for writing assignments

- booklet patterns

- games and puzzles that support learning in curriculum areas such as math, science, and writing

- activity sheets that help students organize information, respond to learning, and explore topics in a meaningful way

- patterns for projects that connect to holidays, special occasions, and commemorative events

All year long, you can weave the ideas and reproducible patterns in these unique books into your monthly lesson plans and classroom activities. Happy teaching!

# What's Inside

You'll find that this book is
chock-full of reproducibles
that make lesson planning easier:

■ puppets and
picture props

■ bookmarks,
booklets, and
book covers

■ game boards,
puzzles, and
word finds

■ stationery

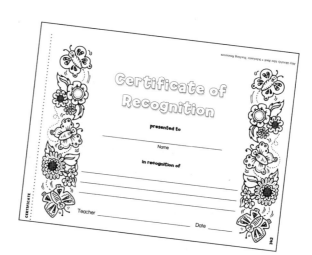

■ awards and certificates

# How to Use This Book

The reproducible pages in this book have flexible use and may be modified to meet your particular classroom needs. Use the reproducible activity pages and patterns in conjunction with the suggested activities or weave them into your curriculum in other ways.

## ★ PHOTOCOPY OR SCAN

To get started, think about your developing lesson plans and upcoming bulletin boards. If desired, carefully remove the pages you will need. Duplicate those pages on copy paper, color paper, tagboard, or overhead transparency sheets. If you have access to a scanner, consider saving the pattern pages as PDF files. That way, you can size images up or down and customize them with text to create individualized lessons, center-time activities, interactive whiteboard lessons, homework pages, and more.

## ★ LAMINATE FOR DURABILITY

Laminating the reproducibles will help you extend their use. If you have access to a roll laminator, then you already know how fortunate you are when it comes to saving time and resources. If you don't have a laminator, clear adhesive vinyl covering works well. Just sandwich the pattern between two sheets of vinyl and cut off any excess. Then try some of these ideas:

- Put laminated sheets of stationery in a writing center to use for handwriting practice. Wipe-off markers work great on coated pages and can easily be erased with dry tissue.

- Add longevity to calendars, weather-related pictures, and pocket chart rebus pictures by preserving them with lamination.

- Transform picture props into flannel board figures. After lamination, add a tab of hook-and-loop fastener to the back of the props and invite students to adhere them to the flannel board for storytelling fun.

- To enliven magnet board activities, affix sections of magnet tape to the back of the picture props. Then encourage students to sort images according to the skills you're working on. For example, you might have them group images by commonalities such as initial sound, habitat, or physical attributes.

## ★ BULLETIN BOARDS

### 1. Set the Stage

Use background paper colors that complement many themes and seasons. For example, the dark background you used as a spooky display in October will have dramatic effect in November, when you begin a unit on woodland animals or Thanksgiving.

While paper works well, there are other background options available. You might also try fabric from a colorful bed sheet or gingham material. Discontinued rolls of patterned wallpaper can be purchased at discount stores. What's more, newspapers are easy to use and readily available. Attach a background of comics to set off a lesson on riddles, or use grocery store flyers to provide food for thought on a bulletin board about nutrition.

### 2. Make the Display

The reproducible patterns in this book can be enlarged to fit your needs. When we say enlarge, we mean it! Think BIG! Use an overhead projector to enlarge the images you need to make your bulletin board extraordinary.

If your school has a stencil press, you're lucky. The rest of us can use these strategies for making headers and titles.

- ■ Cut strips of paper, cloud shapes, or cartoon bubbles. They will all look great! Then, by hand, write the text using wide-tipped permanent markers or tempera paint.

- ■ If you must cut individual letters, use 4- by 6-inch pieces of construction paper. (Laminate first, if you can.) Cut the uppercase letters as shown on page 14. No need to measure, as somewhat irregular letters will look creative, not messy.

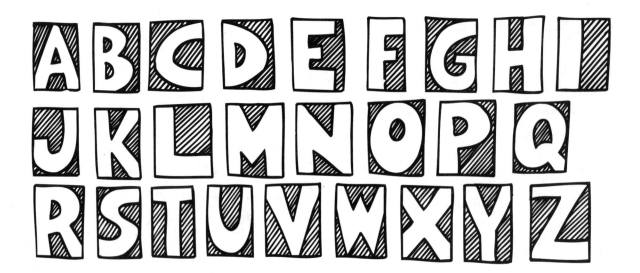

## 3. Add Color and Embellishments

Use your imagination! You'll be surprised at the great displays you can create.

- ■ Watercolor markers work great on small areas. On larger areas, you can switch to crayons, color chalk, or pastels. (Lamination will keep the color off of you. No laminator? A little hairspray will do the trick as a fixative.)

- ■ Cut character eyes and teeth from white paper and glue them in place. The features will really stand out and make your bulletin boards engaging.

- ■ For special effects, include items that provide texture and visual interest, such as buttons, yarn, and lace. Try cellophane or blue glitter glue on water scenes. Consider using metallic wrapping paper or aluminum foil to add a bit of shimmer to stars and belt buckles.

- ■ Finally, take a picture of your completed bulletin board. Store the photos in a recipe box or large sturdy envelope. Next year when you want to create the same display, you'll know right where everything goes. You might even want to supply students with pushpins and invite them to recreate the display, following your directions and using the photograph as support.

## Staying Organized

Organizing materials with monthly file folders provides you with a location to save reproducible activity pages and patterns, along with related craft ideas, recipes, and magazine or periodical articles.

If you prefer, use file boxes instead of folders. You'll find that with boxes there will plenty of room to store enlarged patterns, sample art projects, bulletin board materials, and much more.

# Meeting the Standards

## CONNECTIONS TO THE COMMON CORE STATE STANDARDS

The Common Core State Standards Initiative (CCSSI) has outlined learning expectations in English/Language Arts, among other subject areas, for students at different grade levels. In general, the activities in this book align with the following standards for students in grades K–3. For more information, visit the CCSSI website at www.corestandards.org.

### Reading: Foundational Skills

*Print Concepts*
- RF.K.1, RF.1.1. Demonstrate understanding of the organization and basic features of print.

*Phonics and Word Recognition*
- RF.K.3, RF.1.3, RF.2.3, RF.3.3. Know and apply grade-level phonics and word analysis skills in decoding words.

*Fluency*
- RF.K.4. Read emergent-reader texts with purpose and understanding.
- RF.1.4, RF.2.4, RF.3.4. Read with sufficient accuracy and fluency to support comprehension.

### Writing

*Production and Distribution of Writing*
- W.3.4. Produce writing in which the development and organization are appropriate to task and purpose.
- W.K.5, W.1.5, W.2.5, W.3.5. Focus on a topic and strengthen writing as needed by revising and editing.

*Research to Build and Present Knowledge*
- W.K.7, W.1.7, W.2.7. Participate in shared research and writing projects.
- W.3.7. Conduct short research projects that build knowledge about a topic.
- W.K.8, W.1.8, W.2.8, W.3.8. Recall information from experiences or gather information from provided sources to answer a question.

*Range of Writing*
- W.3.10. Write routinely over extended time frames (time for research, reflection, and revision) and shorter time frames (a single sitting or a day or two) for a range of discipline-specific tasks, purposes, and audiences.

### Speaking & Listening

*Comprehension and Collaboration*
- SL.K.1, SL.1.1, SL.2.1. Participate in collaborative conversations with diverse partners about grade-level topics and texts with peers and adults in small and larger groups.
- SL.K.2, SL.1.2, SL.2.2, SL.3.2. Recount or describe key ideas or details from a text read aloud or information presented orally or through other media.
- SL.K.3, SL.1.3, SL.2.3, SL.3.3. Ask and answer questions about what a speaker says in order to gather additional information or clarify something that is not understood.

*Presentation of Knowledge and Ideas*
- SL.K.4, SL.1.4, SL.2.4. Describe people, places, things, and events with relevant details, expressing ideas and feelings clearly.
- SL.K.5, SL.1.5, SL.2.5, SL.3.5. Add drawings or other visual displays to stories or recounts of experiences when appropriate to clarify ideas, thoughts, and feelings.

### Language

*Conventions of Standard English*
- L.K.1, L.1.1, L.2.1, L.3.1. Demonstrate command of the conventions of standard English grammar and usage when writing or speaking.
- L.K.2, L.1.2, L.2.2, L.3.2. Demonstrate command of the conventions of standard English capitalization, punctuation, and spelling when writing.

*Knowledge of Language*
- L.2.3, L.3.3. Use knowledge of language and its conventions when writing, speaking, reading, or listening.

*Vocabulary Acquisition and Use*
- L.K.4, L.1.4, L.2.4, L.3.4. Determine or clarify the meaning of unknown and multiple-meaning words and phrases based on grade level reading and content, choosing flexibly from an array of strategies.
- L.K.6, L.1.6, L.2.6, L.3.6. Use words and phrases acquired through conversations, reading and being read to, and responding to texts.

# CALENDAR TIME

## Getting Started

| | | | May | | | |
|---|---|---|---|---|---|---|
| Sunday | Monday | Tuesday | Wednesday | Thursday | Friday | Saturday |
| | | | | | | |
| | | | | | | |
| | | | | | | |
| | | | | | | |
| | | | | | | |

19

CALENDAR

### ★ MARK YOUR CALENDAR

Make photocopies of the calendar grid on page 19 and use it to meet your needs. Consider using the write-on spaces to:

- write the corresponding numerals for each day

- mark and count how many days have passed

- track the weather with stamps or stickers

- note student birthdays

- record homework assignments

- communicate with families about positive behaviors

- remind volunteers about schedules, field trips, shortened days, and so on

## ★ CELEBRATIONS THIS MONTH

Whether you post a photocopy of pages 20 though 23 near your class calendar or just turn to these pages for inspiration, you're sure to find lots of information on them to discuss with students. To take celebrating and learning a step further, invite the class to add more to the list. For example, students can add anniversaries of significant events and the birthdays of their favorite authors or historical figures.

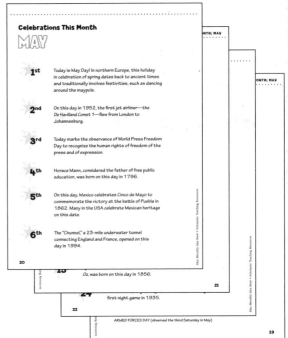

## ★ CALENDAR HEADER

You can make a photocopy of the header on page 24, color it, and use it as a title for your classroom calendar. You might opt to give the coloring job to a student who has a birthday that month. The student is sure to enjoy seeing his or her artwork each and every day of the month.

## ★ BEFORE INTRODUCING WHAT'S THE WEATHER?

Make a photocopy of the body template on page 25. Laminate it so you can use it again and again. Before sharing the template with the class, cut out pieces of cloth in the shapes of clothing students typically wear this month. For example, if you live in a warm weather climate, your May attire might include shorts and t-shirts. If you live in chillier climates, your attire might include a scarf, hat, and coat. Fit the cutouts to the body outline. When the clothing props are made, and you're ready to have students dress the template, display the clothing. Invite the "weather helper of the day" to tell what pieces of clothing he or she would choose to dress appropriately for the weather. (For extra fun, use foam to cut out accessories such as an umbrella, sunhat, and raincoat.)

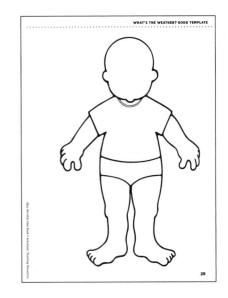

# May

| Sunday | Monday | Tuesday | Wednesday | Thursday | Friday | Saturday |
|--------|--------|---------|-----------|----------|--------|----------|
|        |        |         |           |          |        |          |
|        |        |         |           |          |        |          |
|        |        |         |           |          |        |          |
|        |        |         |           |          |        |          |
|        |        |         |           |          |        |          |

## Celebrations This Month

# MAY

**1st** Today is May Day! In northern Europe, this holiday in celebration of spring dates back to ancient times and traditionally involves festivities, such as dancing around the maypole.

**2nd** On this day in 1952, the first jet airliner—the *De Havilland Comet 1*—flew from London to Johannesburg.

**3rd** Today marks the observance of World Press Freedom Day to recognize the human rights of freedom of the press and of expression.

**4th** Horace Mann, considered the father of free public education, was born on this day in 1796.

**5th** On this day, Mexico celebrates Cinco de Mayo to commemorate the victory at the battle of Puebla in 1862. Many in the USA celebrate Mexican heritage on this date.

**6th** The "Chunnel," a 23-mile underwater tunnel connecting England and France, opened on this day in 1994.

*May Monthly Idea Book* © Scholastic Teaching Resources

**7th** English poet Robert Browning was born on this day in 1812.

**8th** Today is World Red Cross and Red Crescent Day, observed on the birthday of Red Cross founder, Henry Dunant.

**9th** Mother's Day was recognized as a national holiday for the first time on this day in 1914.

**10th** On this day in 1869, a gold spike was driven into the tracks at Promontory Summit, Utah, marking the completion of the Transcontinental railroad.

**11th** Irving Berlin, American composer and songwriter, was born on this day in 1888.

**12th** International Nurses Day is celebrated on this day, the anniversary of Florence Nightingale's birthday.

**13th** Joe Louis, former heavyweight boxing champion of the world, was born on this day in 1914.

**14th** Jamestown, the first English settlement in America, was established in Virginia on this day in 1607.

**15th** Lyman Frank Baum, author of *The Wonderful Wizard of Oz*, was born on this day in 1856.

**16**th  On this day in 1975, Junko Tabei became the first woman to reach the summit of Mount Everest.

**17**th  The first Kentucky Derby was held on this day in 1875.

**18**th  On this day in 1980, an earthquake triggered the eruption of Mount St. Helens, a volcano in the state of Washington.

**19**th  The Ringling Brothers Circus opened on this day in 1884.

**20**th  Dolley Madison, former First Lady of the United States, was born on this day in 1768.

**21**st  Charles Lindburgh successfully completed the first solo flight across the Atlantic Ocean on this day in 1927.

**22**nd  Today is International Day for Biological Diversity.

**23**rd  Today is World Turtle Day, a day on which the American Tortoise Rescue calls attention to turtles and tortoises.

**24**th  In Cincinnati, Major League Baseball held its very first night game in 1935.

**25th** The award-winning movie, *Star Wars*, was released on this day in 1977.

**26th** On this day in 1927, the 15 millionth *Model T Ford* car was driven out of the factory—on its last day of production.

**27th** American biologist Rachel Carson, whose books inspired the environmental movement, was born on this day in 1907.

**28th** On this day in 1937, the Golden Gate Bridge in San Francisco, California, officially opened to traffic.

**29th** Sir Edmund Hillary and Tenzing Norgay became the first humans to reach the summit of Mount Everest on this day in 1953.

**30th** The dedication ceremony for the Lincoln Memorial was held on this day in 1922.

**31st** On this day in 1859, Big Ben—London's world-famous clock—went into operation.

Other important occurrences this month include:

INTERNATIONAL LABOR DAY OR WORKERS' DAY (May 1)

MOTHER'S DAY (observed the second Sunday in May)

ARMED FORCES DAY (observed the third Saturday in May)

May

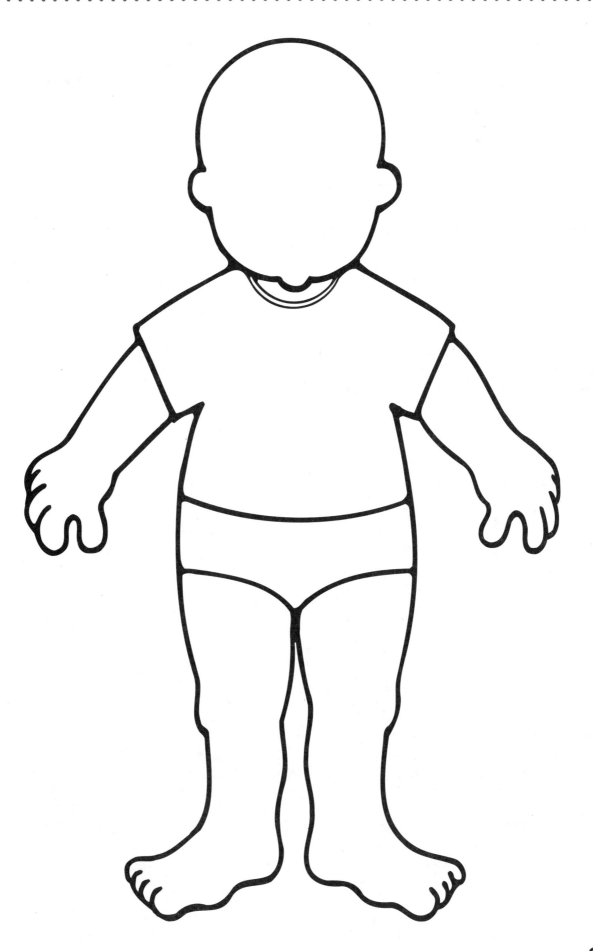

# PLANTS AND FLOWERS

Plants play an important role in the natural environment. Human and other animal life could not exist without plants

In the food chain, all animals rely on plants. Herbivores eat plants to survive. Omnivores, like most people, eat plants and animals. Carnivores eat the herbivores and omnivores. Finally, microscopic plants and animals return what's left of the carcasses to the soil after the scavengers are done. It's a cycle dependent on plant life. (Beyond food, humans rely heavily on plants for industry in the production of textiles, building materials, and medicine.)

Plants also help provide the oxygen we need to breathe and, in turn, live. They take in water and minerals from the soil and carbon dioxide from the air. Sunlight, which gives plants energy, is absorbed through the leaves and allows the plant to process these elements into oxygen. This process of changing inorganic matter into organic matter is called photosynthesis.

## May Day

Typically celebrated on May 1st, May Day acknowledges the rebirth and revival of life that the spring season brings after the harshness of winter. In ancient times, the Romans offered bouquets of flowers to Flora, their goddess of spring, during the festival called *Floralia*. Though Roman political influence waned over time, many of their traditions remained and have been integrated into European cultures. The advent of the Maypole and the crowning of the May Queen is one such example.

## Plant Life

Tap the inspiration of May Day to teach students about the importance of plants in our world. To introduce the topic, invite students to share what they already know. Include in your discussion that plants come in many different shapes, sizes, and colors. For instance, the smallest plant is a one-celled algae that can only be seen with a microscope. The tallest is a 300-foot California redwood. Also share that some plants grow in shady, moist environments, while others thrive in hot, dry, desert heat. All plants have attributes that make them unique—from fragrant leaves or showy blooms of vibrant colors to fruit, berries, or seeds.

## Suggested Activities

### ★ FLOWER WORD FIND

Start out your unit with the word find (page 30) to introduce students to names of flowers. To take vocabulary building a step further, invite students to brainstorm other flower names and flower-related terms. Then post the words from the word find, along with words that students have brainstormed, on a May word wall, and encourage students to use some of the words in their creative writing.

### ★ PARTS-OF-A-FLOWER DIAGRAM

As a group, discuss the parts of a flower (petal, pistil, sepal, stamen, and stem), and their corresponding functions and locations. Then distribute photocopies of the flower diagram (page 31) for students to complete. Explain that they may utilize resources on the Internet, in the classroom, at the school library, and within the community to label their diagrams. (Garden clubs can be a helpful resource.) For online research about flower anatomy, consider having children visit www.enchantedlearning.com and search the topic "plants." Finally, use the answer key (page 143) to check students' labeled diagrams.

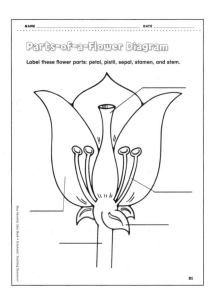

## ★ SEED SCIENCE

Explain that students will be doing some research and scientific observation related to seeds they choose to plant and grow. As the days and weeks pass, students can record observations about their plant's light and water needs and physical attributes, such as sprouts, leaves, and flowers. Provide photocopies of pages 32–36, soil, spoons, flowerpots, water, and a choice of seeds (such as flower, fruit, vegetable, and herb). Have students staple their gardening report pages together and then plant their seeds to get started.

## ★ MATCHING FLOWERS AND POTS

Make several photocopies of the patterns on page 37 to create matching activities, such as letter recognition, math facts, antonyms, and words and definitions. First, record the words, math facts, or images you'd like students to match on the flower and flowerpot pairs. Cut the slits in the flowerpots and attach to a garden-themed bulletin board. Then glue a craft stick to the back of each flower stem to make it sturdy. Have students complete the matching activity by tucking each flower into the slit of its corresponding flowerpot.

## ★ PRACTICE! PRACTICE! PRACTICE!

Complement your studies by creating color-coded flowers to help students practice developing skills. To begin, make a copy of page 38. Label the sections of the flower with math problems, numbers, short vowel words, or any other skill you want students to practice. Add a color key for students to follow. For example, the key might direct students to color all even-numbered sums (for addition problems) green. After programming, make a class supply of the page to distribute to students.

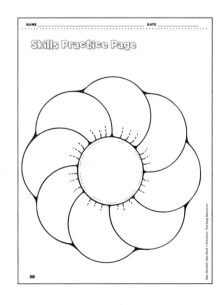

## ★ BLOOMING BULLETIN BOARD

This flowery display will make students "bloom" with pride. Copy a supply of the flower patterns (page 39) for students to color and cut out. Have them glue the center cutout to the flower and add the leaves. Or, you might have students attach photos of themselves in the center of their flowers, or write their names in bold marker. Arrange the flowers and leaves on a bulletin board to create a warm, May welcome for visitors to the class.

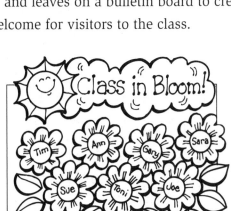

## ★ MAY DAY CARDS

Usher in spring with these floral greeting cards. Students can write special messages, greetings, or poems inside their cards. (These work well as Mother's Day cards!) Or, students might use their cards as mini-book covers by stapling paper to the inside and trimming the pages to fit. To get started, photocopy the patterns on pages 40–41 (one per child). Provide color construction paper and have students do the following:

1. Fold the construction paper in half so that the two short sides meet.

2. Choose a flower pattern. Glue it along the folded edge of the construction paper where indicated.

3. Cut out the flower shape through both layers of the construction paper.

4. Color the flower as desired.

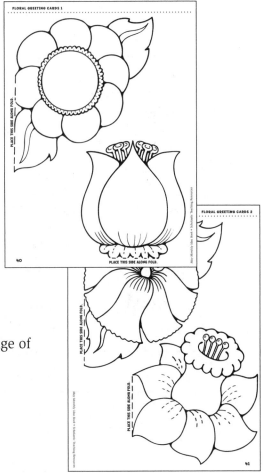

# Flower Word Find

## Find these words in the puzzle below:

ASTER   BLUEBELLS   BOUGAINVILLEA   CROCUS   DAFFODIL
HEATHER   IRIS   MARIGOLD   POPPY   VIOLET   YARROW   ZINNIA

```
G N M K L O P L K M K N E G A S W E R T X
A C W D V F M N F V K E S E D F T G H Y U
Z R I E I D A F F O D I L I N A T A B N B
Q O S D C R R C K E T Y A R C U S T O M N
A M E R A V I T Z Y Y E N S C Y H R G D J
A R N B O U G A I N V I L L E A A R T Y Y
X T C L A F O R N O I T L W E R C B F M I
Q I X U D B L F N M O S H A L R I D I R U
A L D E I H D E I B L M E S P O P P Y T E
Z L X B O G T F A R E F A P S W N B S M U
A A F E S E R A P E T H T S T M I E T C T
W O S L L J P L O R N S H D R C R S A Y N
M T D L A P S E N O R R E F G R I S W E R
A R A S T E R C V J A C R O C U S H J K L
```

Write about the kind of flowers that live near you. If you need
more space to write, use the back of this page.

_____

_____

_____

_____

May Monthly Idea Book © Scholastic Teaching Resources

# Parts-of-a-Flower Diagram

**Label these flower parts: petal, pistil, sepal, stamen, and stem.**

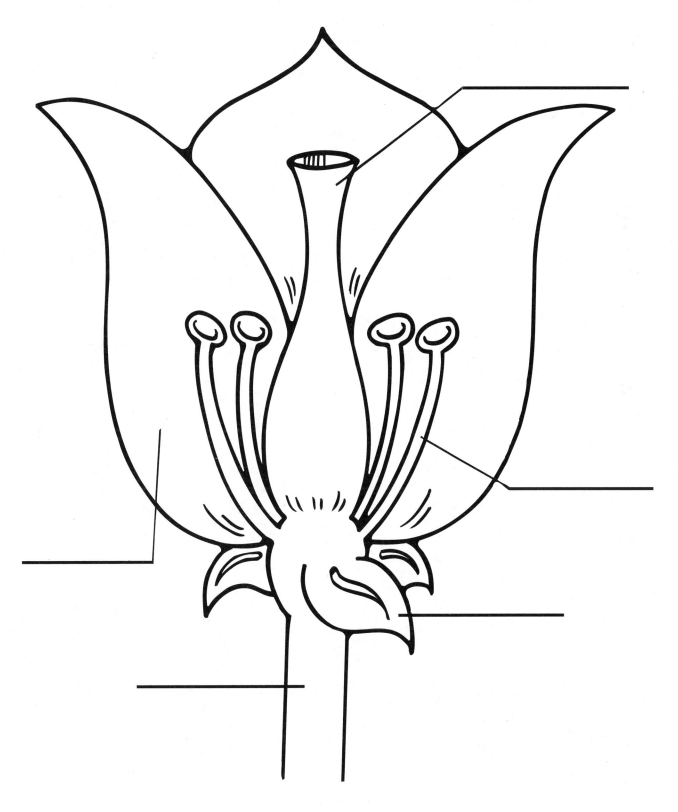

# My Gardening Report

_____
**Name**

_May Monthly Idea Book_ © Scholastic Teaching Resources

# Planting Seeds

I chose this type of seed: _____

My plant will be a:

❏ flower    ❏ fruit    ❏ vegetable    ❏ herb

❏ _____

Here are the directions to plant the seeds: _____

_____

Date I planted my seeds: _____

It will grow to be about this tall: _____

Plants need water.

Here is my watering schedule.

| Week | Sunday | Monday | Tuesday | Wednesday | Thursday | Friday | Saturday |
|------|--------|--------|---------|-----------|----------|--------|----------|
| 1. |  |  |  |  |  |  |  |
| 2. |  |  |  |  |  |  |  |
| 3. |  |  |  |  |  |  |  |
| 4. |  |  |  |  |  |  |  |
| 5. |  |  |  |  |  |  |  |
| 6. |  |  |  |  |  |  |  |

Check off each day you water your plant.

# Plant Parts

Label each plant part. Write a definition for each one.

BUD    FLOWER    LEAF    STEM    ROOTS

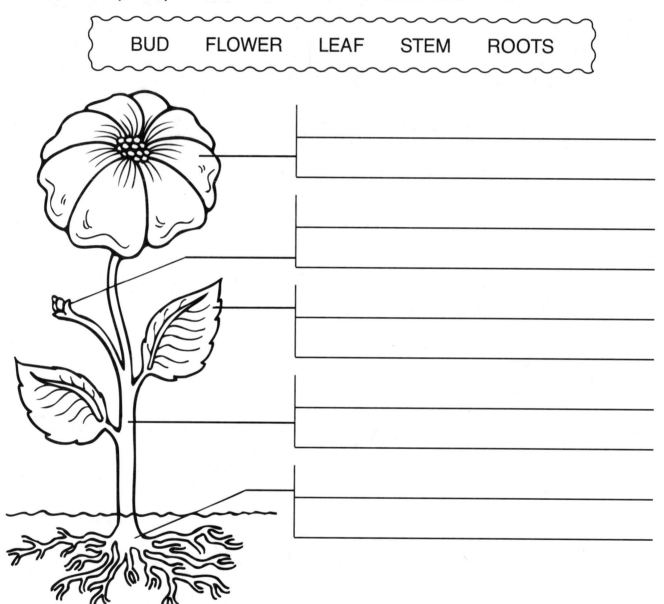

Tell about the light needs of your plant.

_____

_____

*May Momtity Idea Book* © *Scholastic Teaching Resources* • 34

# Observations

Draw pictures of your plant.

1. This is my plant after it sprouted.

2. This is my plant after _____ days.

3. This is my plant after _____ days.

4. This is my plant fully grown.

# Observations

My plant was this tall on these dates:

Height Units                    Date

_____  ❏ inches  ❏ cm        _____

_____  ❏ inches  ❏ cm        _____

_____  ❏ inches  ❏ cm        _____

_____  ❏ inches  ❏ cm        _____

_____  ❏ inches  ❏ cm        _____

Here is a description of my plant:

_____

_____

_____

4

# Skills Practice Page

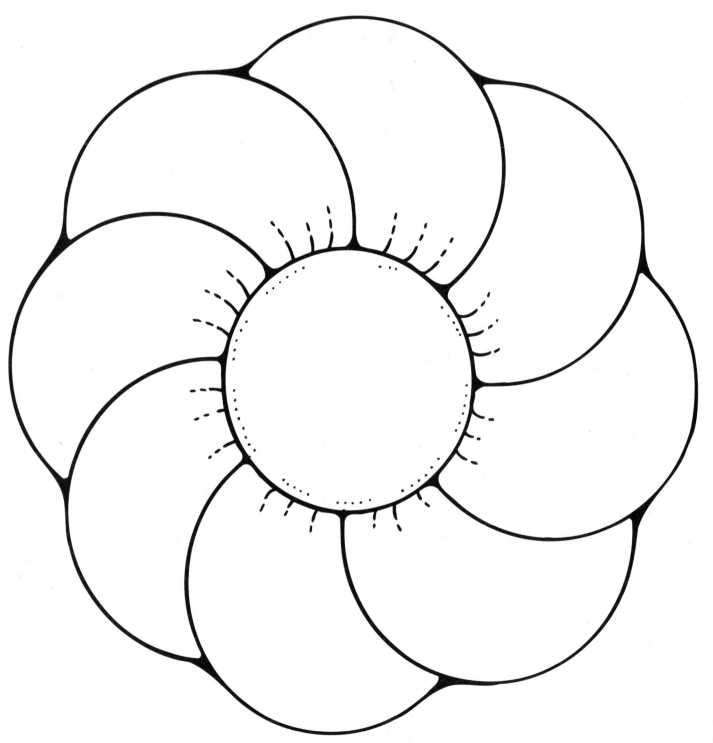

*May Monthly Idea Book* © Scholastic Teaching Resources

PLACE THIS SIDE ALONG FOLD.

**PLACE THIS SIDE ALONG FOLD.**

*May Monthly Idea Book* ©Scholastic Teaching Resources

# MEXICO

Familiar to many of us simply as Mexico, the United Mexican States is a country in North America that has a rich cultural history with origins dating back tens of thousands of years. When more complex cultures and societies developed, many civilizations including the Maya and Aztec emerged.

## Maya

In the large southern regions of Mexico and Central America, Maya civilization flourished over 2,000 years ago. The people built grand cities and huge architectural structures known as temples. They also produced paintings, pottery, and sculpture. In addition, they developed an accurate calendar as well as advancements in the sciences of astronomy and mathematics.

## Aztec

The Aztecs were an advanced civilization that ruled a large empire in central Mexico before the Spanish conquest. It was the Aztec people that founded the city of Tenochtitlan, which was established on an island in the middle of a large lake. The Aztecs built raised earthen roads linking the island to the mainland. Later the site became the capital of Mexico, Mexico City.

## Cinco de Mayo

The tiny town of Puebla, Mexico, was the site of an important battle on May 5, 1862. Over six thousand French soldiers had come to take the village. But, with a small army of just two thousand brave people, the Mexicans defeated the French in the Battle of Puebla. This victory showed the world that the Mexican people would fight to keep their country and their freedom. At the war's conclusion, General Zaragosa sent a report to President Benito Juarez that stated, "The Mexican army has covered itself with glory!" Today *Cinco de Mayo*, a holiday that celebrates the Mexican heritage, is observed in both Mexico and the United States.

## Suggested Activities

## ★ SPANISH WORD FIND

Distribute copies of the word find (page 46) to students. Explain that the word bank contains Spanish words associated with the Mexican culture. Below the puzzle is an activity in which students match facts about Mexico. After students complete the activities, challenge them use Spanish-English dictionaries and other sources to define each word from the puzzle. They can write their definitions on the back of the page.

## ★ NATIONAL PRIDE

There is much cultural imagery associated with Mexico, but two of the most well known are the iconic Mexican Hat Dance and the national flag. Show students a photocopy of the dancers on page 47. Explain that the Mexican Hat Dance is a modern folk dance that gained popularity after the Mexican Revolution. In modern Mexico, the dance is considered a favorite traditional dance that celebrates national pride. The dance itself involves a pair or several pairs of dancers, a sombrero, and participants stamping and tapping rhythmically to festive music. Invite students to research other aspects of the Mexican people and culture that interest them.

Afterward, explain that the Bandera de México—or Mexican flag—is also a symbol of national pride. Display a color image of the flag. Point out that from left to right, the color bands are green, white, and red. The national coat of arms is in the white center band of the flag. Encourage students to research the Mexican flag to learn more about what its colors and the coat of arms symbolize.

To wrap up, distribute copies of pages 47–48 for students to color and use as props when sharing what they've learned about Mexico, its people, and culture.

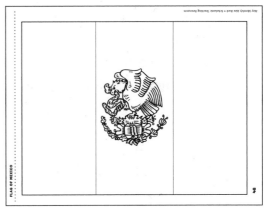

## ★ RESEARCHING AND WRITING ABOUT MEXICAN CULTURE

Divide the class into several groups and explain that each group will research different aspects of Mexican life. Then assign a different topic (food, clothing, language, agriculture, dance, music, and so on) to each group. Have students use books available in the classroom, as well as library books, Internet resources, and other sources, such as videos and personal interviews, to learn about their topic.

Ask groups to research past and present information about their topic. For example, younger students might research food or clothing from the past and present; older students might investigate the role and types of music in today's culture compared to that in the past. Students interested in the Maya culture might look at the Smithsonian National Museum of Natural History's link to Unmasking the Maya (http://anthropology.si.edu/maya/). If students are interested in learning about indigenous languages in Mexico, you can direct them to a page developed by the Houston Institute for Culture: http://www.houstonculture.org/mexico/aztec.html. Regardless of the topic, most students will need a few days to complete this assignment well. When students are ready to publish their writing, provide them with copies of the South-of-the-Border stationery (page 49) for their final text. Finally, invite volunteers to share their research with the class.

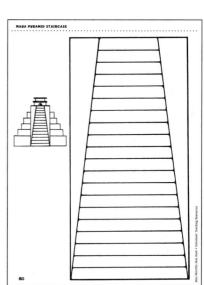

## ★ MAYA PYRAMID

To add a period backdrop for students' research related to the Maya culture, especially the temples and pyramids, enlarge the Maya pyramid staircase, on page 50. Have students color and cut out the staircase, then ask them to work together to assemble the rest of the pyramid on a bulletin board, using images of actual Maya pyramids as a model. (Or they might refer to the small image on page 50.) If desired, students can embellish the pyramid with beads, stickers, or other craft items. Invite students to post facts, interesting information, and their writings about the Maya culture on the display.

## ★ THE AZTEC CALENDAR STONE

The Aztec's sun god, Tonatiuh, is featured on the center of the Aztec Calendar Stone, perhaps the most famous Aztec sculptures known to exist. Other carvings on the stone, which measures twelve feet in diameter, are believed to represent days of the month and symbols of the universe. To acquaint students with the sculpture, use page 51 for a math-skills practice page. First, color, cut out, and program a copy of the image by labeling each rectangular shape on it with a number. Choose numbers that serve as answers to addition or subtraction problems. Then prepare cards with corresponding problems for students to solve, writing answers on the back for self-checking purposes. The activity works best when you laminate all of the pieces. To use, students solve each problem, use a wipe-off marker to check off that answer on the calendar stone, then check the back of the problem card to see if they chose the correct answer.

## ★ SPANISH BINGO

Celebrate Spanish, the official language of Mexico, with this Bingo game. Copy and cut out the word cards on page 52. Make several copies of the game board (page 53). Using the word cards as a reference, write a different mix of Spanish words in the boxes on each game board. Laminate the word cards and game boards for durability. Then supply players with Bingo chips, distribute the game boards, and invite students to learn Spanish words as they play the game.

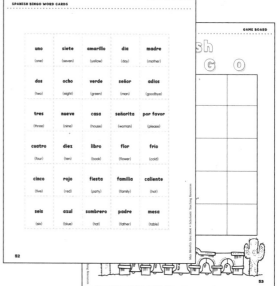

## ★ FIESTA FINGER PUPPETS

Hold a fiesta to wrap up your study of Mexico. For snacks, prepare traditional foods, such as quesadillas or nacho chips for students to enjoy. Invite them to dress in traditional costumes or create crafts of the culture. Also, bring in recordings of Mexican music, such as the music for the Mexican Hat Dance. For fun, distribute copies of the finger puppets (page 54) for students to color, cut out, and "dance" around while enjoying the music. Or they might use the puppets as props to share what they've learned about Mexico.

**45**

# Spanish Word Find

## Find these Spanish words in the puzzle below:

ADIOS   CASA   ESPAÑOL   FIESTA   HACIENDA

MESA   PIÑATA   SEÑOR   SEÑORITA

SERAPE   SOMBRERO   TORTILLA

```
G Ñ M K L O P L K M K Ñ E G A S W E R T X
A S W D V F R Ñ F V K E S E D F T G H Y U
Z R I E I D S E D R A W P I Ñ A T A B Ñ B
Q T S D C R I C K E T Y A R C U S T O M Ñ
A O E R A V B T H Y Y E Ñ S C V H R G D J
A R Ñ A T C O A D S E Ñ O R I T A R T Y Y
X T C O A F E R T O I T L W E C C B F M I
Q I X C D B G F D M E S A A L A I D I R U
A L D F I H X E R B Y M O S Q U E T E T E
Z L X C O G T F R R D F G P S D N B S M U
A A F F S E R A P E R H E S T I D E T C T
W O S X L J P L O R Ñ S C D R C A S A Y Ñ
M T D Ñ A P S E Ñ O R R T F G R D S W E R
A S D E R Q X C V J A Z U A T Y Ñ H J K L
```

## Draw lines to match these facts about Mexico.

the capital of Mexico ●               ● Maya

Cinco de Mayo ●               ● Mexico City

one of many
ancient civilizations ●               ● the fifth of May

May Monthly Idea Book © Scholastic Teaching Resources

*May Monthly Idea Book* © Scholastic Teaching Resources

*May Monthly Idea Book* © Scholastic Teaching Resources

# Aztec Calendar Stone

| | | | | |
|---|---|---|---|---|
| **uno**<br><br>(one) | **siete**<br><br>(seven) | **amarillo**<br><br>(yellow) | **dia**<br><br>(day) | **madre**<br><br>(mother) |
| **dos**<br><br>(two) | **ocho**<br><br>(eight) | **verde**<br><br>(green) | **señor**<br><br>(man) | **adios**<br><br>(goodbye) |
| **tres**<br><br>(three) | **nueve**<br><br>(nine) | **casa**<br><br>(house) | **señorita**<br><br>(woman) | **por favor**<br><br>(please) |
| **cuatro**<br><br>(four) | **diez**<br><br>(ten) | **libro**<br><br>(book) | **flor**<br><br>(flower) | **frio**<br><br>(cold) |
| **cinco**<br><br>(five) | **rojo**<br><br>(red) | **fiesta**<br><br>(party) | **familia**<br><br>(family) | **caliente**<br><br>(hot) |
| **seis**<br><br>(six) | **azul**<br><br>(blue) | **sombrero**<br><br>(hat) | **padre**<br><br>(father) | **mesa**<br><br>(table) |

*May Monthly Idea Book* © Scholastic Teaching Resources

# Spanish

# BINGO

Free!

Cut out.

Cut out.

Cut out.

Cut out.

# MOTHER'S DAY

In May of 1905, Miss Anna M. Jarvis encouraged her church in Grafton, West Virginia, to dedicate a church service in honor of her mother who had passed away three years earlier. Because her mother had loved carnations, Anna presented everyone in attendance with one of her special flowers. Red carnations were given to honor mothers who were living and white carnations for those who had passed on. The following year, Miss Jarvis campaigned for establishing a special day to honor all mothers. She began her campaign by writing letters to members of Congress and other important people. Several states soon declared a day to be set aside as Mother's Day, usually celebrated on a Sunday in the month of May. Carnations continued to be associated with this special day. On May 9, 1914, President Woodrow Wilson announced the first Mother's Day Proclamation, in which a day should be observed to express "our love and reverence for the mothers of our country."

Today, Mother's Day is celebrated on the second Sunday in May. In many parts of the world, this event is observed on different dates. In every case, the holiday offers an opportunity to show gratitude and remembrance, to express love and appreciation, for all mothers and mother figures. While you explore this holiday with students, be sure to communicate reverence for all women who offer the kindnesses of a mother's love.

## Suggested Activities

 ## FAMILY WORD FIND

Distribute a photocopy of the word find (page 59) to each student. Explain that the word bank contains words associated with family. Then invite students to find and circle each word in the puzzle. Finally, have each student use words from the puzzle to write about an important woman in his or her life.

## ★ A MOTHER'S DAY TEA

Help students and families set aside a special time to honor the women who are important to them, whether they are mothers, grandmothers, aunts, or even neighbors. To prepare a special "tea" for this purpose, fill in a copy of the invitation (page 60). Then make a class supply for students to color and take home. In advance, involve students in planning the event. For example, they might help prepare foods and activities. Here are some suggestions:

- Make and serve brewed tea in teapots and iced tea in pitchers.

- Make and serve tea sandwiches or cookies.

- Read poetry and literary excerpts about families.

- Sing songs or play tranquil musical selections.

## ★ JUST-FOR-YOU MINI-BOOK

Invite students to make customized mini-books for the special mothers (or mother figures) in their lives. First, make double-sided photocopies of the mini-book (pages 61–62). Explain that students can make the book for their mother or other significant women in their lives (such as a grandmother, aunt, or sister). If desired, they can prepare these and present them at the Mother's Day tea party. (See above.) Be sure to provide enough copies for each student to make one mini-book for each of his or her guests. Have students follow these directions to make their mini-book:

1. Fold the page in half, so the cover (featuring the wreath) is on the outside. Draw a picture of the person on the wreath and write her name on the line.

2. Draw pictures and write responses on pages 2–4 where indicated.

3. Embellish the pages with color and craft items, such as lace and plastic jewels.

Invite volunteers to share their mini-books with the class before taking them home to present to the recipients. Or, display the mini-books for your class tea, where attendees can read and enjoy them. Be sure to set aside a time for students to present the books to their special guests.

## ★ PRESENTS FOR MOM

One way for students to honor Mother's Day traditions is through the giving of small gifts. Many cultures offer such tokens to show appreciation of mothers. Following are some simple gifts that students can make to give to the special woman (or women) in their lives.

### Scented Sachets

Invite students to make sachets to give as gifts. Ask volunteers to explain why sachets are so often found in drawers and closets. Then distribute the materials (see list at right). To make a sachet, have students place a cotton ball in the center of the square netting and sprinkle the cotton with scented powder or cologne. Then demonstrate how to gather the four corners together and tie with a ribbon. No doubt, Mom will find a spot for these!

> **MATERIALS**
> (for each sachet)
> • 8-inch square of nylon netting
> • cotton ball
> • scented powder or cologne
> • 12-inch length of cloth ribbon

### Doorknob Bouquet Basket

These easy-to-make baskets slip over a doorknob and add cheer to any space. Students can fill them with fresh or hand-made flowers (see Paper-Flower Pledges, below). To make, have students color and cut out tagboard copies of the pattern on page 63. As needed, help them cut the slits inside the flower. Then demonstrate how to fold the sides together, as shown, and tape or staple them in place.

### Paper-Flower Pledges

Students can make these flowers to fill their doorknob bouquet baskets (above), or to present individually to their special "mom." They might label the stems with redeemable pledges (such as chores they will do), special messages, words of wisdom, or their "mom's" favorite quotes. To make the flowers, distribute copies of page 64 and have students do the following:

**1.** Cut out and color each flower.

**2.** Write their selected text on the stems.

**3.** Add embellishments such as glitter, silk flowers, or felt.

## GREETING CARDS

Children love making cards, and moms love receiving them!
Here are some cards kids are sure to enjoy making for the
special "mom" in their lives.

### 3-D Daisy Greeting Card

Photocopy the flower patterns on page 65 in several vibrant
colors (two copies per student). Distribute the patterns, a sheet
of construction paper, and a 6- to 8-inch length of green yarn
to each student. Then have students cut out their patterns,
fold their construction paper in half (for the card), and do the
following:

1. Fold up the petals of both flowers. Glue one flower near
   the top of the card, gluing only the center in place. Glue
   the other flower on top of the first one, staggering the petals.

2. Glue both circles to the center of the flower.

3. To make a stem, glue on the green yarn.

4. Fold each leaf along the line. Glue the leaves to the stem,
   gluing only one side of each leaf to the card.

5. Write a Mother's Day greeting on the outside of the card
   and a special message on the inside.

### Roses-Are-Red Greeting Card

These special cards can conceal secret sentiments! Distribute
copies of the rose patterns (page 66) for students to color and
cut out. Demonstrate how to attach the leaves to the rose with
a brass fastener (as shown), checking that the leaves open and
close easily over the flower. Then invite students to write a
special sentiment, rhyme, riddle, or other message on the back
of their leaves. To use, the reader opens the leaves and flips the
flower over to read the message.

# Family Word Find

**Find these words in the puzzle below:**

AUNT    BABY    BROTHER    COUSIN    FATHER    FRIEND

GRANDFATHER    GRANDMOTHER    MOTHER    NEIGHBOR

NEPHEW    NIECE    SISTER    UNCLE

```
G  N  M  K  L  O  P  L  K  M  K  N  E  G  A  S  W  E  R  T  X
A  B  W  N  V  F  R  N  F  N  E  I  G  H  B  O  R  G  H  Y  U
F  R  I  E  N  D  X  E  D  R  A  W  P  I  A  A  T  A  S  N  B
Q  O  S  P  C  R  I  C  K  E  T  Y  G  R  B  U  S  T  I  M  N
A  T  E  H  A  V  B  T  H  Y  Y  E  R  S  Y  V  H  R  S  D  J
A  H  N  E  T  C  O  A  D  S  E  N  A  R  I  A  U  N  T  P  Y
X  E  C  W  A  F  E  R  T  O  I  T  N  W  E  C  C  B  E  M  I
Q  R  X  C  D  B  B  F  G  R  A  N  D  M  O  T  H  E  R  R  U
A  L  C  F  I  H  X  E  R  B  Y  M  F  S  Q  U  E  T  E  T  E
Z  L  O  C  O  G  T  F  R  R  D  F  A  T  H  E  R  B  S  M  U
A  A  U  N  C  L  E  A  P  E  R  H  T  S  T  I  D  E  T  C  T
W  O  S  X  L  J  P  L  O  M  O  T  H  E  R  C  A  S  A  Y  N
M  T  I  N  A  P  S  E  N  O  R  R  E  F  G  R  D  S  W  E  R
A  S  N  I  E  C  E  C  V  J  A  Z  R  A  T  Y  Z  H  J  K  L
```

Using four of the words from the puzzle, write a paragraph about an important woman in your life. If you need more space to write, use the back of this page.

_____

_____

_____

# It's a Tea Party!

We hope you will join us.

Date: _____

Time: _____

Location: _____

# It's a Tea Party!

We hope you will join us.

Date: _____

Time: _____

Location: _____

*May Monthly Idea Book* © Scholastic Teaching Resources

## Just for You!

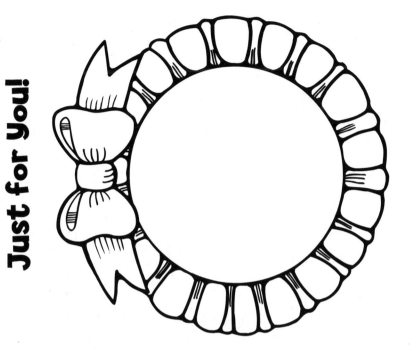

**You are someone special!**

This mini-book was written

especially for you

by

I wrote it on this date:

4

# Favorite Things

My favorite memory with you is

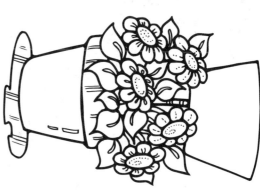

Three words that describe you are:

1.

2.

3.

2

When we're together, I feel

Here's a picture of a present I would like to give to you!

3

*May Monthly Idea Book* © Scholastic Teaching Resources

wash dishes

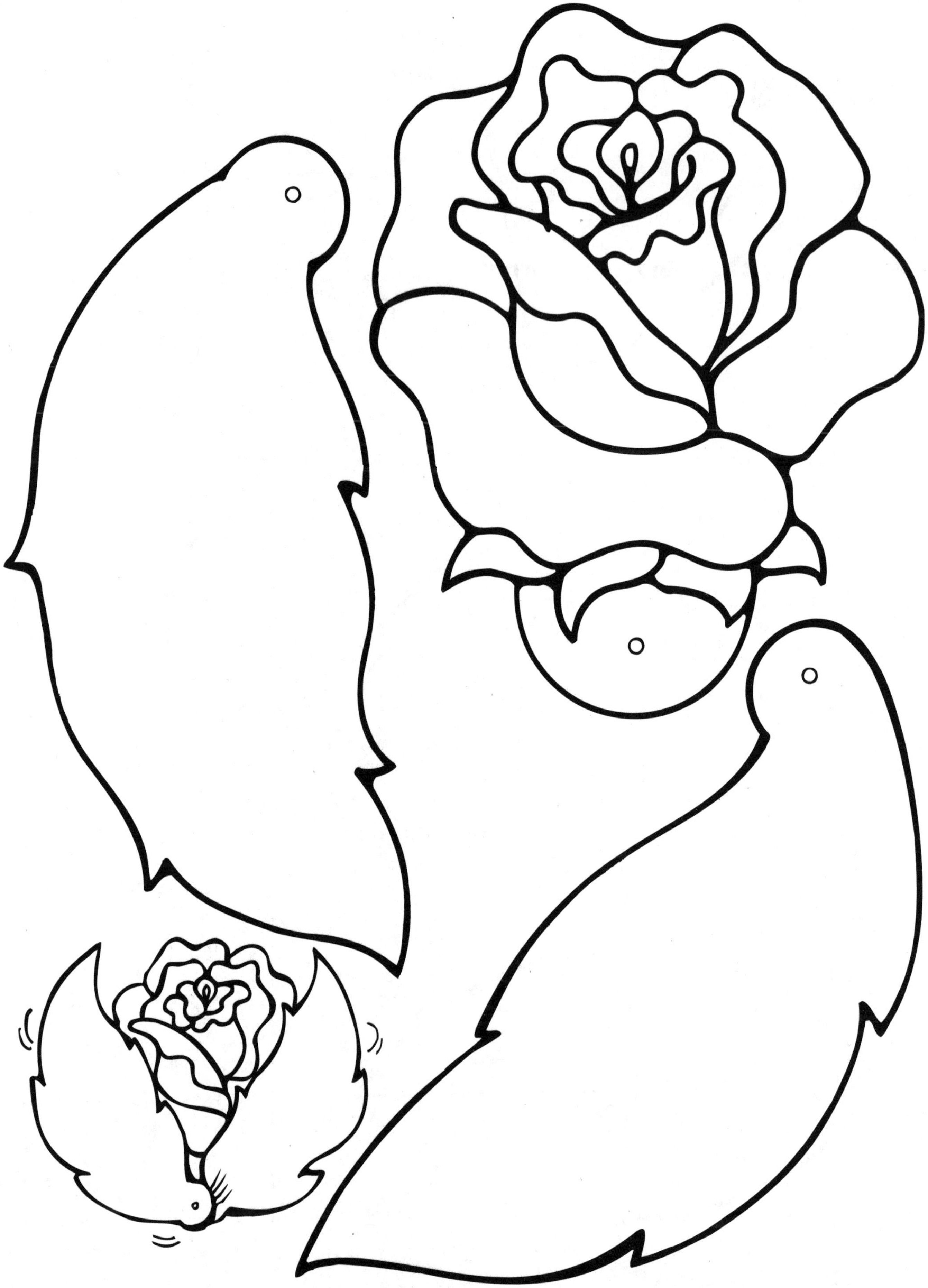

# BIRDS

Found around the world and in all climates, birds are diverse in specialized skills, including flight, song, and migration. While birds are warm-blooded vertebrates with feathers and wings, they are oviparous (lay eggs) like some cold-blooded animals, such as reptiles.

## Observing, Listening, and Learning

Watching and learning to identify birds can be a wonderful hobby that children can enjoy for the rest of their lives. A simple walk through a park or a hike in the woods can become an exciting activity by quietly observing our feathered friends.

Eyes and ears are all students really need to begin bird watching, but a pair of field glasses, or binoculars, can be a big help. You will also want to refer to a bird guidebook to assist children in identifying birds. A small notebook can also come in handy for recording observations and keeping a list of the birds you've encountered as a class. When identifying a bird for the first time, invite students to note characteristics such as its shape, color, size, and its chirp or "song."

You might find these websites helpful in preparing lessons about birds and bird watching:

- ■ **http://birds.audubon.org/** A treasure trove of information is available via this link to the National Audubon Society. You'll find information about birding, bird profiles, links to your state's Audubon site, and much more.

- ■ **http://macaulaylibrary.org/index.do** Don't miss the archive of animal sounds and videos through the Macaulay Library at the Cornell Lab of Ornithology, where you can search the bird you're studying by its common or scientific name and find audio (calls and songs) as well as video segments.

## Suggested Activities

 ## BIRD WORD FIND

This activity helps students build vocabulary while honing their listening skills. To begin, brainstorm words associated with birds. Record students' suggestions on chart paper, then display the list where students can readily add words they encounter in their reading and class discussions. To reinforce students' developing vocabularies, distribute photocopies of the Bird Word Find (page 72) for them to complete. Then invite students to add words from the word find to their list. You can even have volunteers look up definitions of unfamiliar terms and share their findings with the group. Students can use these words in writing assignments about birds.

**67**

## ★ BIRDING BASICS

Begin a discussion about bird watching by inviting volunteers
to brainstorm names and features of birds they've learned about
from their reading, the Internet, television, and other sources. As
a group, discuss the parts of a bird's body and their corresponding
functions. Distribute photocopies of the bird diagram (page 73)
to students. Have them use the words from the box to label the
diagram. Use the Answer Key (page 143) to check students' work.

## ★ BIRD WATCHING BOOKS

Discuss strategies with students for observing birds without
disturbing them. Then explain that students will observe and
write about a specific variety of bird (to be determined by the
birds that are common and active in your immediate area).
Distribute photocopies of the booklet (pages 74–81) for students
to staple together and fill out during and after their observations.
When completed, invites students to share their books with the
class. Afterward, collect the books and assemble them into a
collaborative field guide to place in your class library so students
can enjoy them again and again.

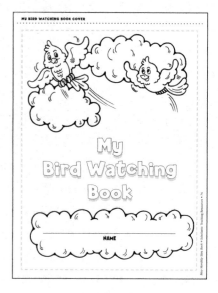

## ★ HANDS-ON NATURE

Ask a member of the local Audubon Society, someone who
raises birds, or a bird caller to visit the classroom. Any of these
specialists will be happy to tell about their profession and may
even be able to bring in live or mounted birds for observation.

If visiting a local park where children can observe birds
personally is more your style, build on students' bird knowledge
by taking a field trip. To liven up the trip, make tagboard
photocopies of the visor pattern (page 82) for students to color
and cut out. Then have them punch a hole at each end, where
indicated, and add a length of elasticized string to fit the visor to
their head. (With elasticized string, students can easily remove
their visors without retying.) Invite students to wear their visors
during their bird-watching field trip. You might explain that the
visors will make it easy for you to spot students while they're out
spotting birds!

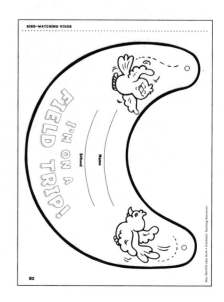

## ★ BIRD FEEDER FUN

Invite students to make and set up several home-made bird feeders. (Recycled milk jugs and cartons work well for this.) Place the feeders in full view of the classroom's windows. Then conduct an experiment by filling each feeder with a different type of bird food, such as millet, sunflower seeds, suet, or cracked corn. You might also consider using peanut butter, peanuts, raisins, breadcrumbs, or small chunks of apples. Ask students to record which feeders attract the most birds. They could also note what time of day the birds are most active and which feed they consume the quickest. Later, have students use their findings in graphing activities.

## ★ EARLY LIFE STAGES

For this sequencing activity, the information below refers specifically to bird egg incubation and stages of development. To get started, make photocopies of the sequencing cards (page 83) and distribute to students. Then have students sequence and glue their cards to a 9- by 18-inch sheet of construction paper as you read the following.

**Card 1:** A female bird lays oval-shaped eggs. The eggs are incubated, typically being warmed by the body heat of one of the parent birds.

**Card 2:** Chicks hatch from their eggs, using a part of their beaks called the egg tooth.

**Card 3:** Before flying, most young birds need time to improve their vision and develop specialized feathers and coordination.

**Card 4:** The young birds or fledglings are ready to fly. Depending on the species, they may also be ready to feed themselves.

Note that some students may use a sequence that differs from the one above. If so, you might invite those students to write a sentence beneath each picture, explaining what is happening. Their narratives will likely be informative, showing their rationale and developing knowledge about the growth stages of birds.

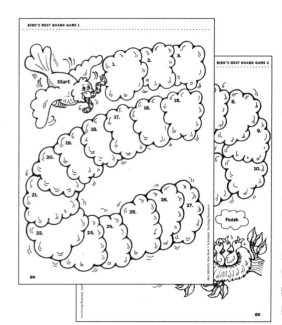

## ★ BIRD'S NEST BOARD GAME

Use this game for a small-group or learning center activity. Or, make several games and divide the class into groups so they can all play at the same time! To get started, photocopy the game boards (pages 84–85). Glue the two parts of the game board together on poster board or to the inside of a file folder. How you use the game and what skills you want students to practice is up to you. Simply write the desired text (or math problems) on the spaces of the game board and create task cards to use with the game. Then color the game board and laminate it for durability.

## ★ BIRD BINGO

You can play this game with the whole class or small groups. Begin by making several photocopies of the game board on page 86. Fill the spaces with bird-related vocabulary words. (You might use some words from the word find on page 72.) Copy the programmed game boards, making enough for each student to have one. Then make a set of caller cards that includes all of the words used on the game boards. Provide Bingo chips or dried beans for students to use as markers, then play the game like a traditional game of Bingo.

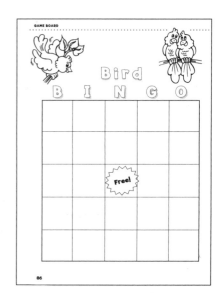

## ★ PAPER BIRDS

Inspired by paper-folding techniques, the bird patterns (page 87) add interest to a writing center—where students can use them to jumpstart or showcase their writing about birds or a related topic. To begin, place photocopies of the patterns in the center along with scissors and several 5- by 26-inch strips of paper. (Bulletin board paper works best for this.) Select a pattern and cut it out. Then demonstrate how to place the pattern at one end of a paper strip and trace it. Fanfold the paper strip, making the folded sections as wide as the pattern and creasing the folds firmly. Cut out the pattern along the solid lines, leaving the folded edges intact. Unfold the strip and show students the repeated bird pattern. Invite volunteers to share ways they might use the patterns in their writing process.

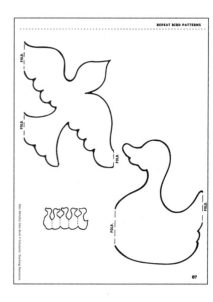

## ⭐ FLYING BIRD MOBILES

Soft breezes from the window will set these bird mobiles aloft. Distribute two photocopies of the pattern (page 88) to each student, along with a 2-foot length of yarn, scissors, a drinking straw, tape, and craft items, such as feathers and sequins. Then have students follow these directions to make a mobile:

**1.** Color and cut out the patterns.

**2.** Fold each bird body in half along the dashed lines. Then cut the slit on each side of the birds.

**3.** Thread a wing cutout through the slits in each bird.

**4.** Thread the yarn through the straw. Use tape to attach each end of the yarn to a bird.

**5.** To make a hanger, tie a length of yarn to the middle of the straw.

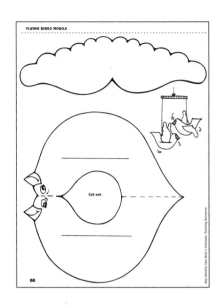

## ⭐ BIRDHOUSE PICTURE PROPS

Make a supply of photocopies of the birds and birdhouse picture props (page 89). Color and cut out the patterns to use for calendar symbols, patterning practice, or matching activities.

## ⭐ A JUST-DUCKY PAGE FRAMER

Showcase students' writing with this "ducky" idea! Photocopy the duck patterns (page 90) for students to color and cut out. Then have them attach the head and tail to their paper to "frame" it. For added flare, students might add glitter details to the duck's beak and tail feathers.

## ⭐ BIRD BOOK LOGS

Make photocopies of the reading log (page 91) for students to use to record their bird-related reading. Explain that they should select and read books in a variety of genres. After reading each book, have students record the title, author, and illustrator (if applicable) on their reading log. When the logs are complete, invite volunteers to tell about their favorite book on the list and share their reading recommendations. After all, a good bird (book) in the hand is worth two in the bush!

# Bird Word Find

## Find these words in the puzzle below:

CARDINAL    CHICKADEE    FLYCATCHER    GOLDFINCH    GROUSE

LOON    MEADOWLARK    MOCKINGBIRD    ORIOLE    PELICAN

PHEASANT    QUAIL    ROADRUNNER    THRASHER    WREN

```
G N M K L O P M K M K P E G A G W E R T X
A S W D V F R E F V K E S E D R T G H Y U
Z R C H I C K A D E E L P I L O O N B N B
Q T A D C S I D K P T I A R Q U A I L F N
A O R G O R I O L E Y C N S C S H R G L J
A R D A T C O W D S E A O R I E A R T Y Y
X T I O A G O L D F I N C H E C T B F C I
Q I N C D B G A D M E S A A L A H D I A U
A L A F I H X R K B Y M O S Q U R T E T E
Z Y L C M O C K I N G B I R D Y A B S C U
A A F F W E R A P E R H E S T I S E T H T
W O S X R O A D R U N N E R R C H S A E N
M T P H E A S A N T R I T F G R E S W R R
A S D E N Q X C V J A Z U A T Y R H J K L
```

Using four of the words from the puzzle, write a paragraph about a
bird you have seen. Use the back of this page.

*May Monthly Idea Book* © Scholastic Teaching Resources

# Bird Diagram

**Label the parts of the bird. Use the words in the box.**

Back   Beak   Breast   Crown   Eye   Feet   Primary Feathers
Secondary Feathers   Tail Feathers   Throat   Wing

May Monthly Idea Book © Scholastic Teaching Resources

# My Bird Watching Book

NAME

# Bird Watching

Bird watching is a lot of fun, especially if you know what to look for! When looking for birds, move slowly and quietly. Use your eyes and ears. When you see a bird, stand still and watch closely. Try to identify the bird using these guidelines:

- location
- size
- shape
- color
- song or call

It's time to begin your bird watching adventure. When you've seen a bird you'd like to know more about, record your observations about it in this booklet.

Date: _____

Time: _____

Place: _____

_____

Weather Conditions: _____

_____

## Location

Some birds are found at the seashore, while others prefer open fields or wooded areas. In cities, you can find most birds in parks or on playgrounds. Some even like to build their homes under the eaves of tall buildings.

Where did you find your bird?

It was near a . . .

❑ stream, pond, or lake.

❑ woodland or forest.

❑ seashore.

❑ field or meadow.

❑ backyard or park.

❑ _____ .

What was it doing? _____

Did you see your bird's nest?     ❑ Yes     ❑ No

If you saw the nest, describe it: _____

_____

_____

2

## Size

A good way to determine the size of a bird is to compare its size to the size of a familiar bird, like a canary or duck.

How does your bird's size compare to another bird you know?

_____

_____

How does your bird's size compare to the size of the bird pictured below?

❑ It is a little larger.

❑ It is much larger.

❑ It is a little smaller.

❑ It is much smaller.

❑ It is about the same size.

**3.25" long**

**2.5" tall**

# Shape

Think about the shape of your bird's body, tail, legs, and beak.
Check each word that is true for your bird.

Its body is . . .  ❑ long    ❑ short    ❑ plump    ❑ slender

Its tail is . . .   ❑ pointed    ❑ square    ❑ long    ❑ short

Its legs are . . .  ❑ long    ❑ short

Its beak looks like this. (Circle one.)

Make a pencil drawing of your bird.

4

## Color

A bird's body may be very colorful,
or it may have only a few colors.

What are the colors on your bird?

Describe the colors on each part of your bird.

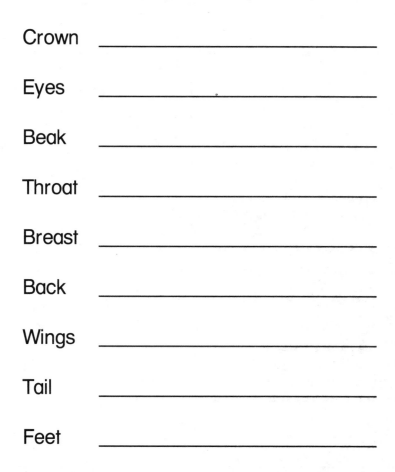

Crown _____

Eyes _____

Beak _____

Throat _____

Breast _____

Back _____

Wings _____

Tail _____

Feet _____

Now add these color details to your bird drawing on page 4.

## Song or Call

Some birds, such as the chickadee, have been named for the sounds they make. Other birds have songs or calls that sound like squeaks, chirps, or squawks. Songbirds are known for their beautiful tunes.

Listen to the sound your bird makes. Describe its song or call.

_____

_____

_____

_____

*May Monthly Idea Book* © Scholastic Teaching Resources • 80

## More About My Bird

I've used my observations and other sources
to identify my bird.

It is a _____.

My bird feeds on: _____

My bird is prey for this animal:

_____

Some more interesting facts about

my bird are: _____

_____

_____

My booklet was completed on:

_____

(date)

I'M ON A FIELD TRIP!

Name

School

*May Monthly Idea Book* © Scholastic Teaching Resources

Start

1.
2.
3.

15.
16.
17.
18.
19.
20.
21.
22.
23.
24.
25.
26.
27.

Finish

# Bird
# B I N G O

| | | | | |
|---|---|---|---|---|
| | | | | |
| | | | | |
| | | Free! | | |
| | | | | |
| | | | | |

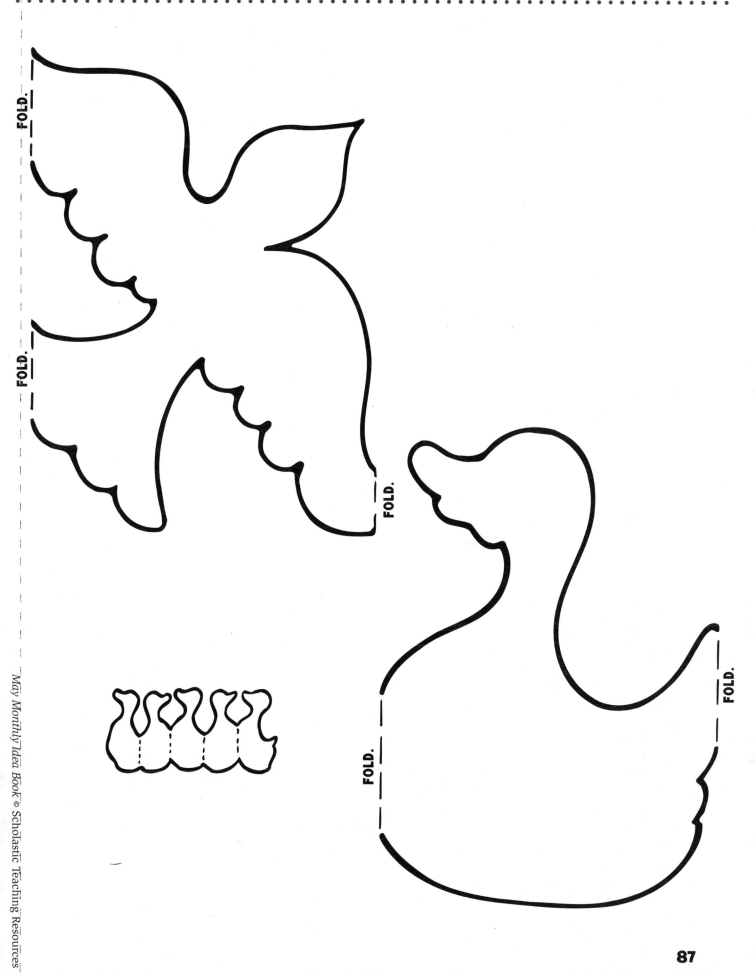

FOLD.

FOLD.

FOLD.

FOLD.

FOLD.

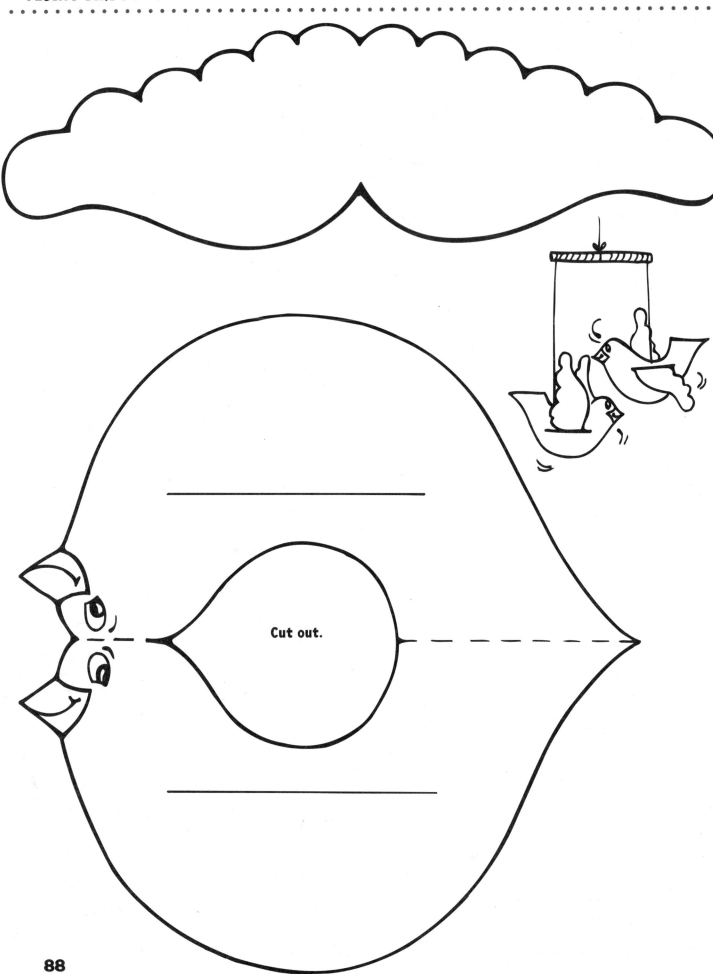

Cut out.

Duck Tales

*May Monthly Idea Book* ©Scholastic Teaching Resources

# Feathered Friends Reading Log

**Biography**  Title _____

Author _____

Illustrator _____

**Fairy Tale**  Title _____

Author _____

Illustrator _____

**Fiction**  Title _____

Author _____

Illustrator _____

**Folk Tale**  Title _____

Author _____

Illustrator _____

**Historical**  Title _____

Author _____

Illustrator _____

**Nonfiction**  Title _____

Author _____

Illustrator _____

# ANIMALS OF AFRICA

The activities and reproducible patterns in this unit are designed to help you teach about the diverse animals in Africa, as well as the habitats in which they live. While rainforests can be found on several continents, Africa's rainforests account for 60 percent of the world's total. Made up of large trees and vines that create a canopy for the underlying plants, the warm, moist rainforest creates an ideal environment in which many animals breed and thrive. Over 40 percent of the land in Africa is grasslands. With the warm climate and varying rainfall, vegetation in the grasslands consists primarily of tall grasses and scattered trees, which suits grazing animals, such as elephants and giraffes.

## Suggested Activities

### ★ ANIMALS-OF-AFRICA WORD FIND

Help students build knowledge about African animals with the word find on page 97. Provide each student with a copy of the puzzle and invite a volunteer to read the words in the word bank. Then have students search the puzzle to find and circle each word. Remind them that the animal names may appear horizontally or vertically and will read from left to right or top to bottom. Reinforce vocabulary by having students use some of the words in a writing assignment.

### ★ FIELD TRIP SAFARI

Arrange a field trip to a zoo or another facility, such as a park or farm, that features African animals. When your preparations have been made, photocopy the field trip form (page 98) to fill out with details and any additional information parents may need to know. Then copy a class supply of the form to send home with students. Emphasize the importance of returning the signed permission slip, explaining that without it, students will not be able to participate in the field trip.

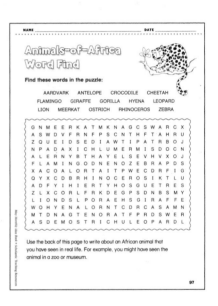

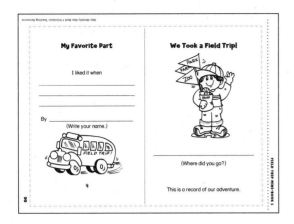

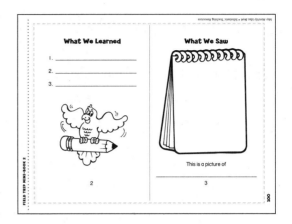

The day before you go on the field trip, list the animals students expect or hope to see. Then, during the trip, encourage students to note the environmental setup for each animal and the food it eats. Back in the classroom, invite students to share their observations. Afterward, copy and distribute double-sided copies of the mini-book on pages 99–100. To complete, ask students to fold the page in half, so the cover (featuring the child with flags) is on the outside. Then have them draw pictures and write responses on the pages where indicated. Finally, invite students to share their mini-books with the class.

## ★ WILDLIFE RESEARCH

With this assignment, students will learn about attributes that make each animal unique. Ask each student to select an African animal to research. Explain that they can use classroom, library, and Internet resources as well as videos, personal interviews, and other helpful sources to gather information about their animal. (The National Wildlife Federation at www.nwf.org might be a useful online resource.)

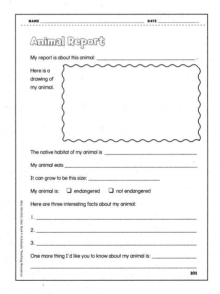

To help students record and organize their findings, distribute copies of the Animal Report on page 101. As a group, discuss ways in which students can find out key information to use in their reports. After they complete their reports, invite volunteers to share their findings. Finally, collect the reports, bind them into a book, and place the book in the class library for students to read and enjoy again and again.

## ★ HABITATS AND INHABITANTS

You can help children learn where to find animals in the wild with this activity that encourages students to learn how the grasslands or savannahs of Africa are different from the tropical regions. To begin, divide the class into two teams and assign a habitat to each one (grasslands or rainforest). Explain that each team will research its habitat and use what students have learned to create a display that shows what kinds of plants live and grow there. Provide students with colored and patterned paper, along with a variety of other materials with which to create and embellish their habitat displays.

Next, students will research what animals live in their habitat. Invite students to add animals to their grassland and rainforest displays. They can create their own animal illustrations or models (using craft items). Or, photocopy a supply of the stand-up animal patterns (pages 102–107) onto tagboard for students to use. Simply have them color and cut out the animal pattern of their choice, then fold the cutout and stand it on a flat surface in front of their habitat display.

## ★ PUPPET PERFORMANCES

Dramatic play is a fun and easy way to add depth to students' investigations of African animals. Invite students to make puppets to use in a performance about these fascinating animals. To prepare, photocopy a supply of the puppet patterns (pages 108–111). Provide students with small paper bags, ask each child to select an animal puppet to make (lion, hippo, or elephant), then have them do the following to complete their puppet:

1. Color the animal patterns with crayons or markers.

2. Cut out the patterns.

3. Glue the animal's head to the flat bottom section of a paper bag. Glue its mouth (or body, for the elephant) to the side of the bag just below the head.

4. Glue on pieces of yarn, feathers, felt, or other craft items to embellish the patterns and add textural interest.

5. To use, slip your hand inside the bag. Use your fingers and thumb to manipulate the bag so that the animal's mouth appears to open and close.

Invite students to use their puppets and the habitat displays (see page 94) as a backdrop for their animal dramatizations. They might act out a situation related to their animals and habitat, or use their puppets to share factual and interesting information about the animals they represent. Alternately, you might read aloud text about particular animals and have students use their puppets to demonstrate actions from the text.

## ★ MONKEY TAILS OF SUCCESS

Photocopy a supply of the monkey-tail notes on page 112. Keep the notes on hand to use as rewards for students who demonstrate effort and positive learning behaviors during your study about African animals and their habitats. To use, write a message of praise or encouragement on a note and present it to the chosen child. Students can cut out their notes and hang them on the edge of their desks, cubby hooks, or bookbag strap. As an added bonus, you might display the note cutouts on an incentive chart or length of yarn strung across the room. The swinging monkeys will be visible for all to see and serve as recognition of students' good work and  efforts.

## ★ GRRREAT WORK!

Roar! This lion will attract attention to exemplary student work. When students have completed quality effort, display their work on the lion page framer (pages 113–114). Photocopy the patterns onto colorful paper and cut out. Also, cut along the lines on the lion's mane. To add a 3-D effect, wrap each section of the mane around a pencil and then release to create a curl. Then glue the lion's head, arms, and tail to the edges of a sheet of construction paper (the body), as shown. Finally, attach a student's work to the page framer to display.

## ★ EXTRAORDINARY ANIMAL POSTERS

Explain that you want students to explore what makes certain animals extraordinary. For research, students will find lots of information on websites of children's museums or zoos, or in resources available in the school or local library. When ready, divide the class into groups. Each group will research a different animal and make a collaborative poster to show what they learn about their animal's unique traits, diet, and habitat.

To get students started, provide poster boards and craft materials. Invite groups to embellish their poster with pictures and diagrams to show what they have learned about their animal. For example, a group may include a giraffe with colored spots to indicate how it uses camouflage on the savannah. Also, if desired, groups might design their poster to take the shape of their animal. If studying the hippo or giraffe, the group might use enlarged copies of the prop patterns on pages 115–116 to use on their poster. Groups studying other animals can create their own patterns, if they'd like to do so. Details such as these will not only add interest to posters, but will help each member of the group shine.

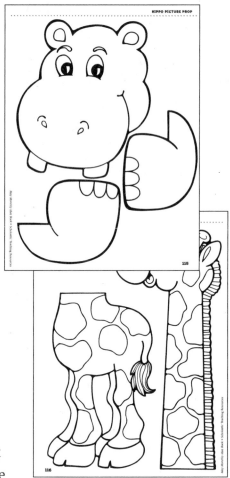

## ★ WRITE-YOUR-OWN ANIMAL STORIES

After students have learned about the unique qualities of several African animals, ask them to write a story that features at least one of these animals. Encourage them to incorporate details in the story that help inform the reader about the facts related to that animal. For instance, if the animal protects itself in a special way or makes an unusual sound, students might describe this in their text. After students complete their final copy, gather their stories to bind into a class book. Add a cover, such as the book cover (page 117) titled, "Amazing African Animals."

# Animals-of-Africa Word Find

## Find these words in the puzzle:

AARDVARK   ANTELOPE   CROCODILE   CHEETAH

FLAMINGO   GIRAFFE   GORILLA   HYENA   LEOPARD

LION   MEERKAT   OSTRICH   RHINOCEROS   ZEBRA

```
G N M E E R K A T M K N A G C S W A R C X
A S W D V F R N F P S C N T H F T A H R U
Z Q U E I D S E D I A W T I P A T R B O J
N P A D A X I C H L U M E R M I S D O C N
A L E R N Y B T H A Y E L S E V H V X O J
F L A M I N G O D N E N O Z E B R A P D S
X A C O A L O R T A I T P W E C D R F I G
Q Y X C D B R H I N O C E R O S I K T L U
A D F Y I H I E R T Y H O S G U E T R E S
Z L X C O R L F R K D E G P S D N B S M Y
L I O N D S L P O R A E H S G I R A F F E
W O H Y E N A L O R N T C D R C A S A M N
M T D N A G T E N O R A T F P R D S W E R
A S D E M O S T R I C H U L E O P A R D L
```

Use the back of this page to write about an African animal that you have seen in real life. For example, you might have seen the animal in a zoo or museum.

# Our Class Is Going on a Field Trip!

Families,

Please sign and return the permission slip below. (Your child must return this signed permission form to participate in the field trip.)

Sincerely,

_____

Teacher

Location: _____

Trip Date/Day of Week: _____

Time Leaving: _____ Time Returning: _____

Additional Details: _____

_____

✂ - - - - - - - - - - - - - - - - - - - - - - - - - - - - - - - - - - - - - - - - - -

# Field Trip Permission Slip

_____

(Today's Date)

I give permission for my child, _____ ,

to go on the field trip to _____ ,

taking place on _____ .

(Day of week and date)

Comments: _____

Parent or Guardian (please print): _____

Phone: _____

Signature: _____

*May Monthly Idea Book © Scholastic Teaching Resources*

# We Took a Field Trip!

PARK
FARM
ZOO
STUFF

_____
(Where did you go?)

This is a record of our adventure.

# My Favorite Part

I liked it when
_____
_____
_____

By _____
(Write your name.)

FIELD TRIP!

4

## What We Learned

1. _____

2. _____

3. _____

2

## What We Saw

This is a picture of _____

3

*May Monthly Idea Book* © Scholastic Teaching Resources

# Animal Report

My report is about this animal: _____ .

Here is a
drawing of
my animal.

The native habitat of my animal is _____

My animal eats _____

It can grow to be this size: _____

My animal is:  ☐ endangered   ☐ not endangered

Here are three interesting facts about my animal:

1. _____

2. _____

3. _____

One more thing I'd like you to know about my animal is: _____

_____

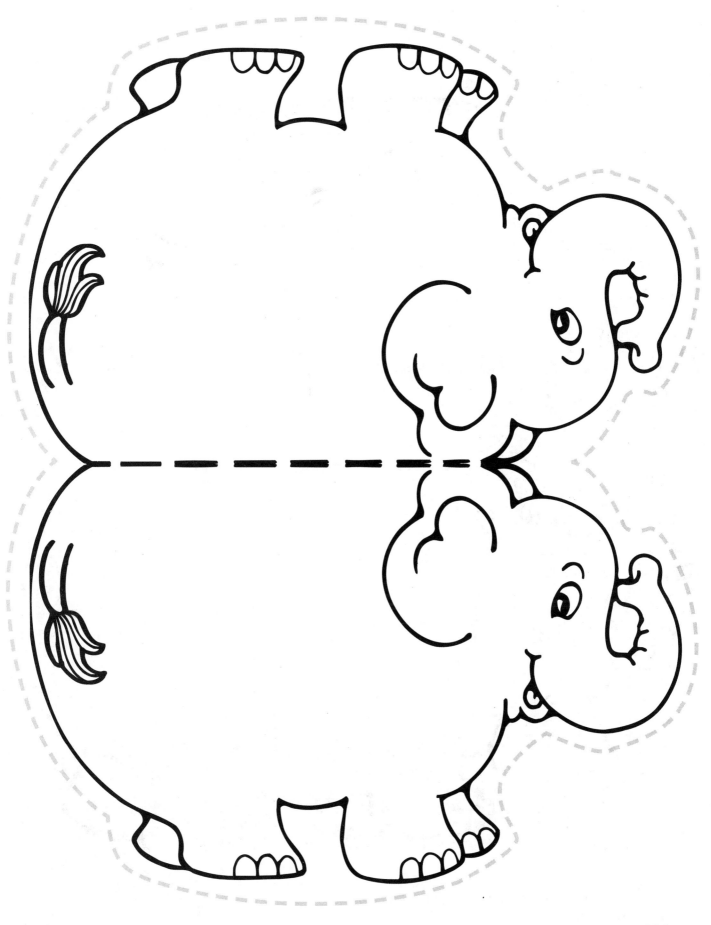

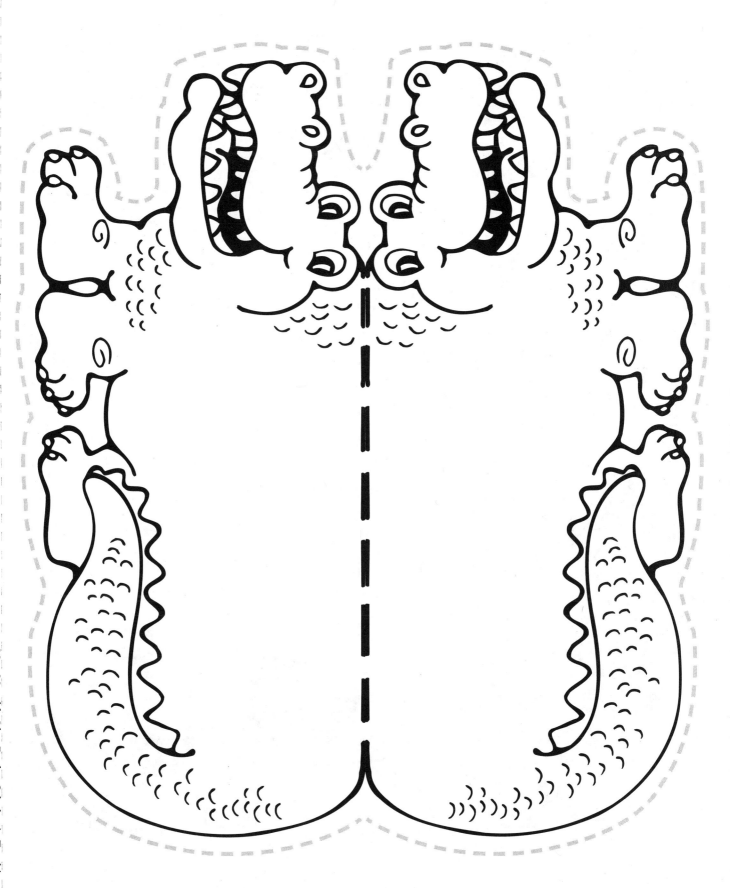

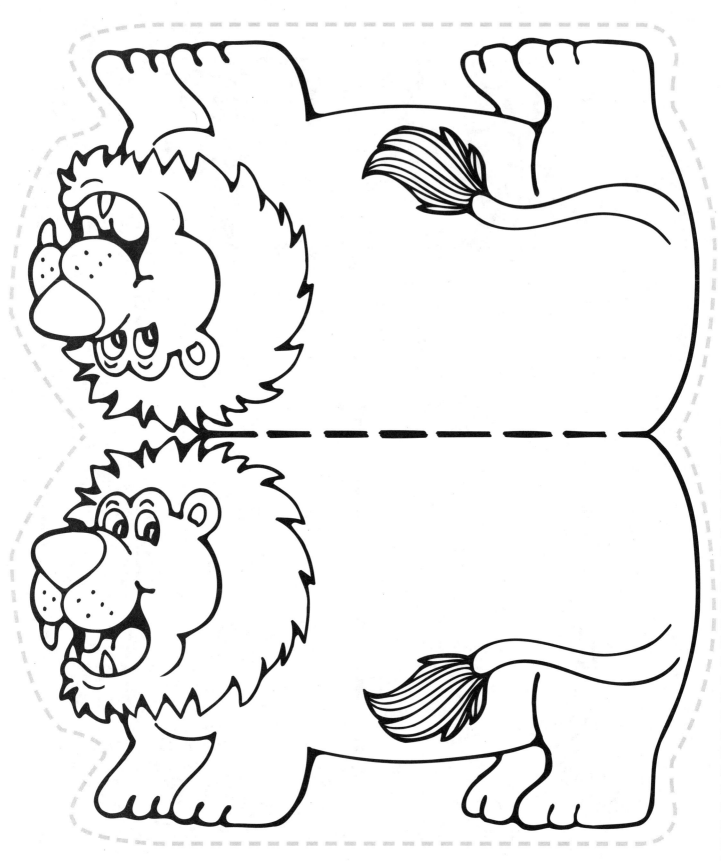

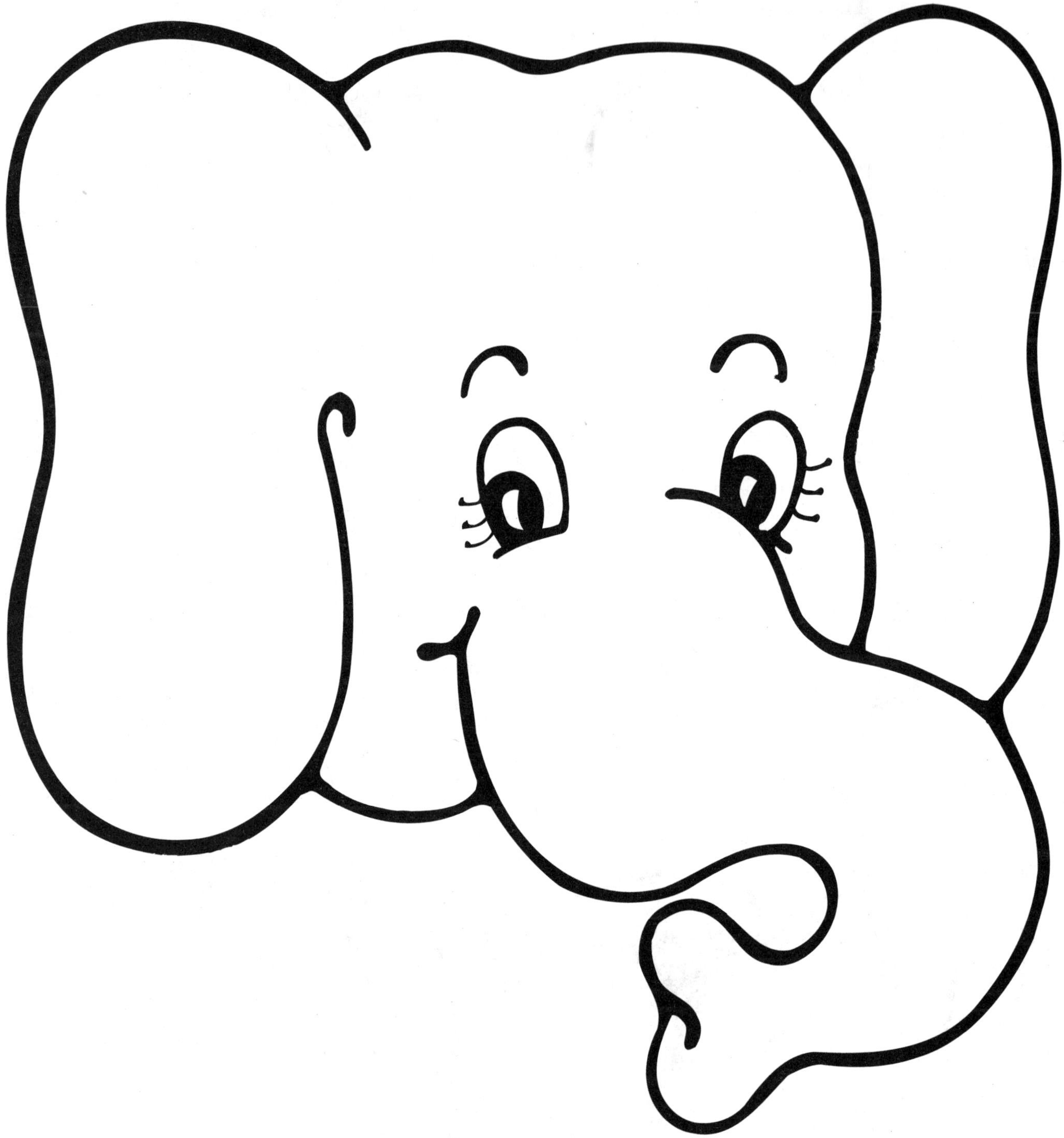

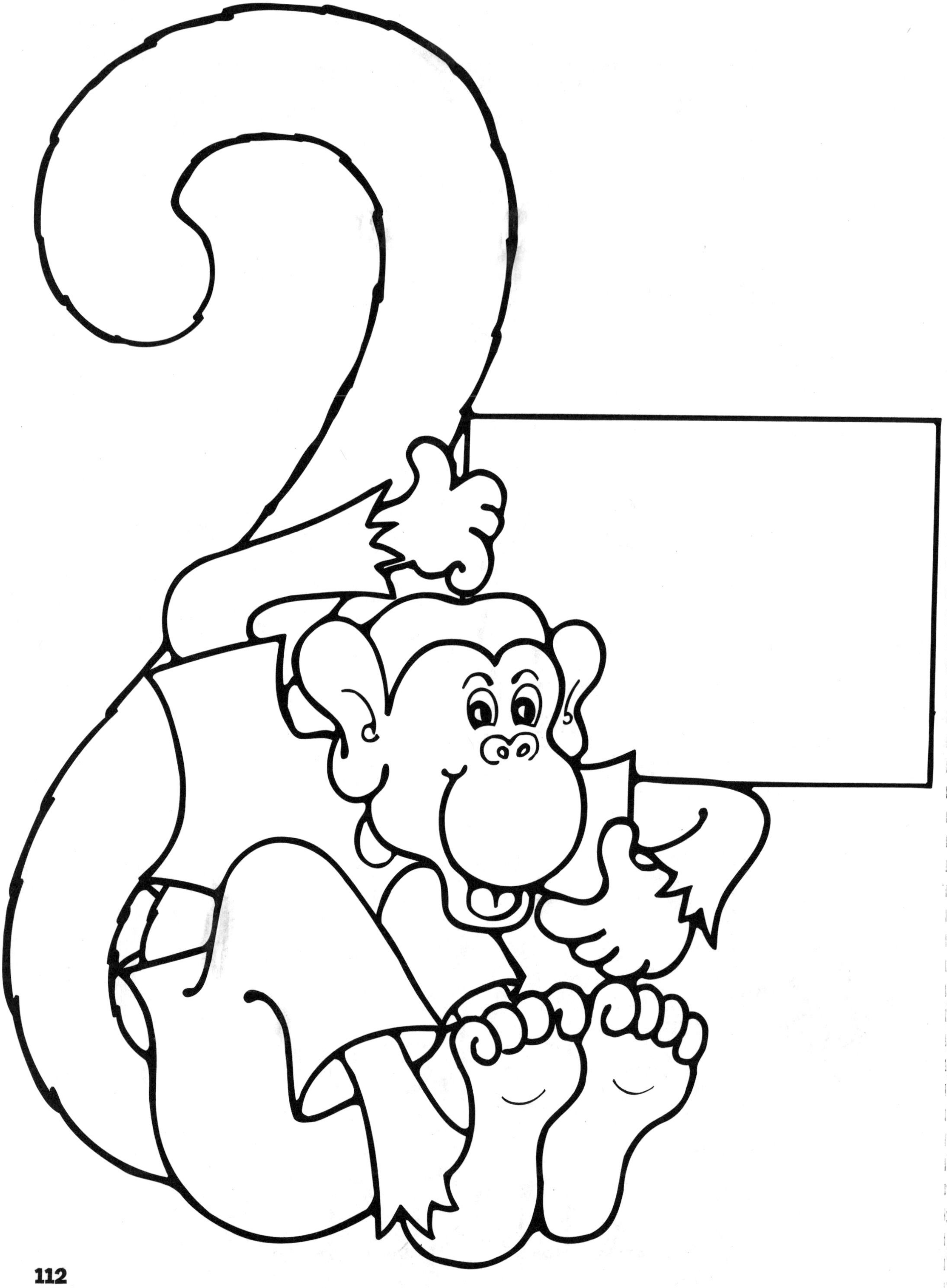

Grrreat Work!

# Amazing African Animals

PLACE THIS SIDE ALONG FOLD.

*May Monthly Idea Book* © Scholastic Teaching Resources

# CIRCUS

Inquiry into circus life invites learning about many topics. For information and free downloadable materials that can help you weave the circus theme with the topics you teach, check out this link to CIRCUSWORKS Education Center, sponsored by Ringling Bros. & Barnum and Bailey Circus: http://www.ringling.com/TextContent.aspx?id = 11778&pa rentID = 390&assetFolderID = 412. You'll find materials and additional links that support curriculum related to geography and diversity, animal care, science, and physical fitness.

## Suggested Activities

### ★ CIRCUS WORD FIND

Invite students to use the Circus Word Find (page 123) to gain familiarity with vocabulary associated with the "big top's" performing arts and live animal shows.

### ★ CLOWN SKILLS WHEEL

Reinforce developing skills with this learning tool that will have students thinking they're just "clowning around" instead of practicing important skills. Provide students with tagboard photocopies of the patterns on pages 124–125, two brass fasteners, and scissors. To make the wheel, have students do the following:

1. Cut out each pattern.
2. Cut out the two rectangular "windows" on the clown. (Younger students may need help with this.)
3. Use a brass fastener to attach the wheel to the back of the clown, as shown.
4. Use a brass fastener to attach the ice-cream cone to the clown's hand where indicated.

To program their wheels, students can write math problems and answers, contractions and their two-word counterparts, or other skills on their wheel by turning it and filling in the boxes behind the window cutouts. When finished, show students how to read the problem through the window on the left side of the wheel and then check their response by moving the ice-cream cone on the right.

## ★ CUSTOMIZED CLOWNS

Distribute photocopies of the clown face patterns (pages 126–127) to students. Encourage them to think about different kinds of clowns as they select, cut out, and glue eyebrows, a nose, and mouth onto their clown to complete its face. If desired, have students use a variety of craft materials to create silly hair and other features to customize their clowns even more. Invite volunteers to tell the class about their clown.

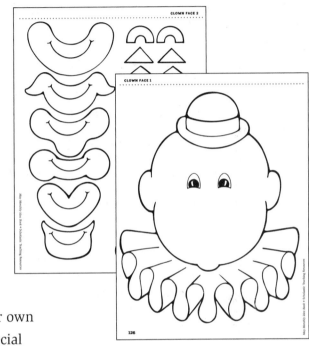

## ★ THREE-RING CIRCUS

Explain that students can plan and perform their own circus acts. You might invite other classes or special guests, such as administrative personnel, special education teachers, or parents, to come and enjoy the show.

### Posters

Like most special events, you'll need to share key information about the occasion. Challenge students to think about what circus signs look like and what information needs to be included. Have the class develop a list of a few important elements to include on their posters (such as *who, what, when,* and *where*). Then distribute photocopies of the Clown and Elephant Picture Props (pages 128–129) to groups for use as poster templates.

When the circus posters are completed, invite volunteers to ask permission to post them at key locations around the school, such as the library, nurse's office, principal's office, and cafeteria.

## Puppets

Puppet performances are a fun way to dramatize what happens in the circus. Invite students to make the following puppets and props for their dramatizations.

**Movable Clown Puppet:** Photocopy and distribute the clown puppet patterns (pages 130–131) to students. Have them use five brass fasteners, where indicated on the patterns, to assemble their puppets. If desired, invite students to glue a wide craft stick to the back of their clown to use as a puppet handle. They can move their clown in a variety of ways to make it dance or to spin and wiggle its limbs in amusing ways. To reinforce good behavior or reward completing assignments, you might award one part of the clown puppet at a time to students when they meet an established goal. When a student has collected all six pieces, he or she can then assemble the puppet.

**Big-Top Finger Puppets:** Distribute photocopies of the finger puppets (pages 132–133) for students to color and cut out. Ask them to carefully cut out the finger holes on their puppets. (Younger students may need help with this.) To use, students simply slip their fingers through the holes to make "legs" for their puppets. Invite students to use their puppets to perform circus acts, share what they know about circuses and different performers, or to tell a circus-related story.

## Scene Setters

Create a "big top" on a class bulletin board or foam display board. To begin, cut a large circus-tent shape from striped wallpaper or brightly colored cloth. Use paper to make a banner for the top of the tent. You might label the banner with your room number, the school's name, or a title, such as "The Big Top." Display the tent prop where children can readily use it as a meaningful backdrop for circus role-playing and dramatizations with their puppets.

## ★ A ROUND OF APPLAUSE

When children have completed outstanding work or demonstrated a lot of effort, display their work with a clown page framer that is sure to bring smiles. Make photocopies of the clown patterns (page 134) onto colorful paper. Then cut out the patterns and color as desired. Glue the clown's head, arms, and feet to the edges of a sheet of construction paper, as shown. Then display a student's work in the center of the page framer.

**CIRCUS FACT BOOKS**

Explain that students will be writing their own
fact books about the circus. Students may enjoy
researching and making a timeline that shows
when different attractions were first featured
at the circus. Invite students to learn about
the origins of our modern day circus. Or, older
students may want to find out how social and
political events have impacted circus life. Here
are other circus-related topics that students
might research:

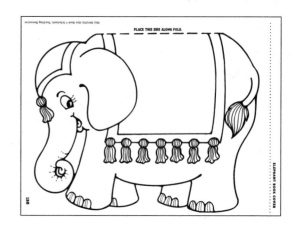

> Emmett Kelley
>
> General Tom Thumb
>
> James Bailey and the Ringling Brothers
>
> Jenny Lind
>
> Joseph Grimaldi
>
> Jumbo the Elephant
>
> The Flying Wallendas
>
> P. T. Barnum

When students complete their writing and are ready to publish, have
them color and cut out a photocopy of the Elephant Book Cover (page
135) to use for their reports. Or, students may enjoy making book covers
of their own design. Whatever they choose, have them title their covers
and add their name as author. Invite volunteers to share a few interesting
facts from their books with the class and make recommendations for
possible areas of further study.

# Circus Word Find

**Find these words in the puzzle below:**

ACROBAT   BALLOONS   BEAR   CIRCUS   CLOWN   FINALE   JUMBO
RINGMASTER   SPOTLIGHT   TAMER   TENT   TIGHTROPE

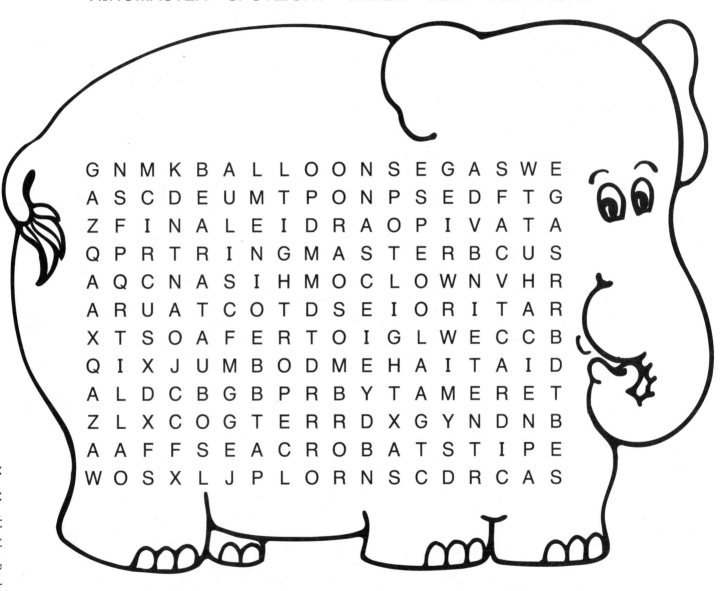

```
G N M K B A L L O O N S E G A S W E
A S C D E U M T P O N P S E D F T G
Z F I N A L E I D R A O P I V A T A
Q P R T R I N G M A S T E R B C U S
A Q C N A S I H M O C L O W N V H R
A R U A T C O T D S E I O R I T A R
X T S O A F E R T O I G L W E C C B
Q I X J U M B O D M E H A I T A I D
A L D C B G B P R B Y T A M E R E T
Z L X C O G T E R R D X G Y N D N B
A A F F S E A C R O B A T S T I P E
W O S X L J P L O R N S C D R C A S
```

**Unscramble each word. Write it on the line.**

nupetsa   _____

norpopc   _____

CUT OUT.

CUT OUT.

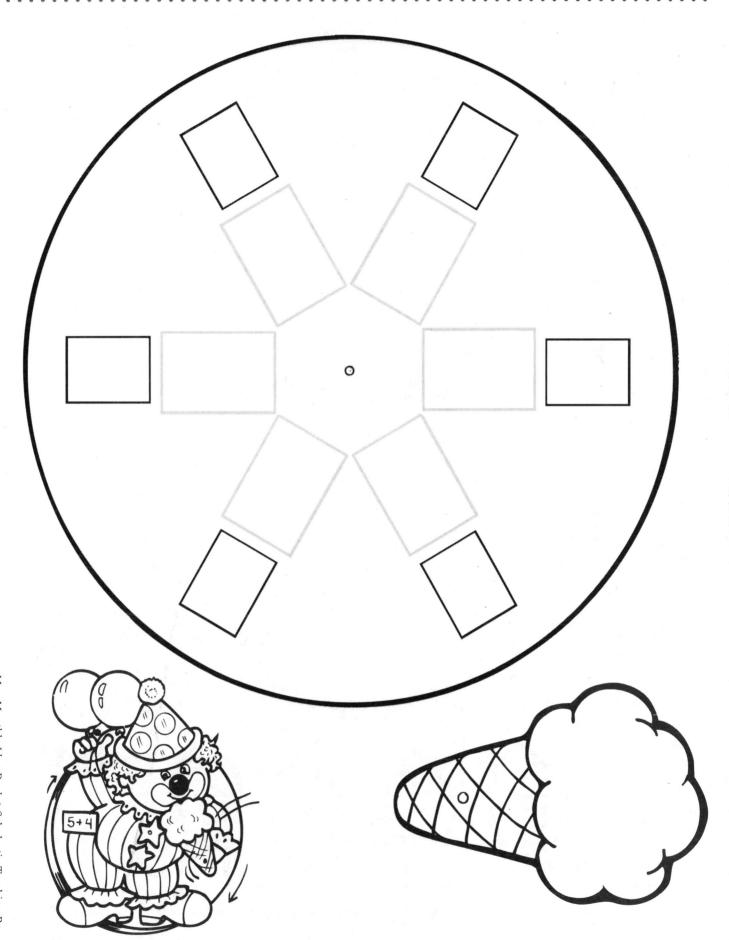

*May Monthly Idea Book* © Scholastic Teaching Resources

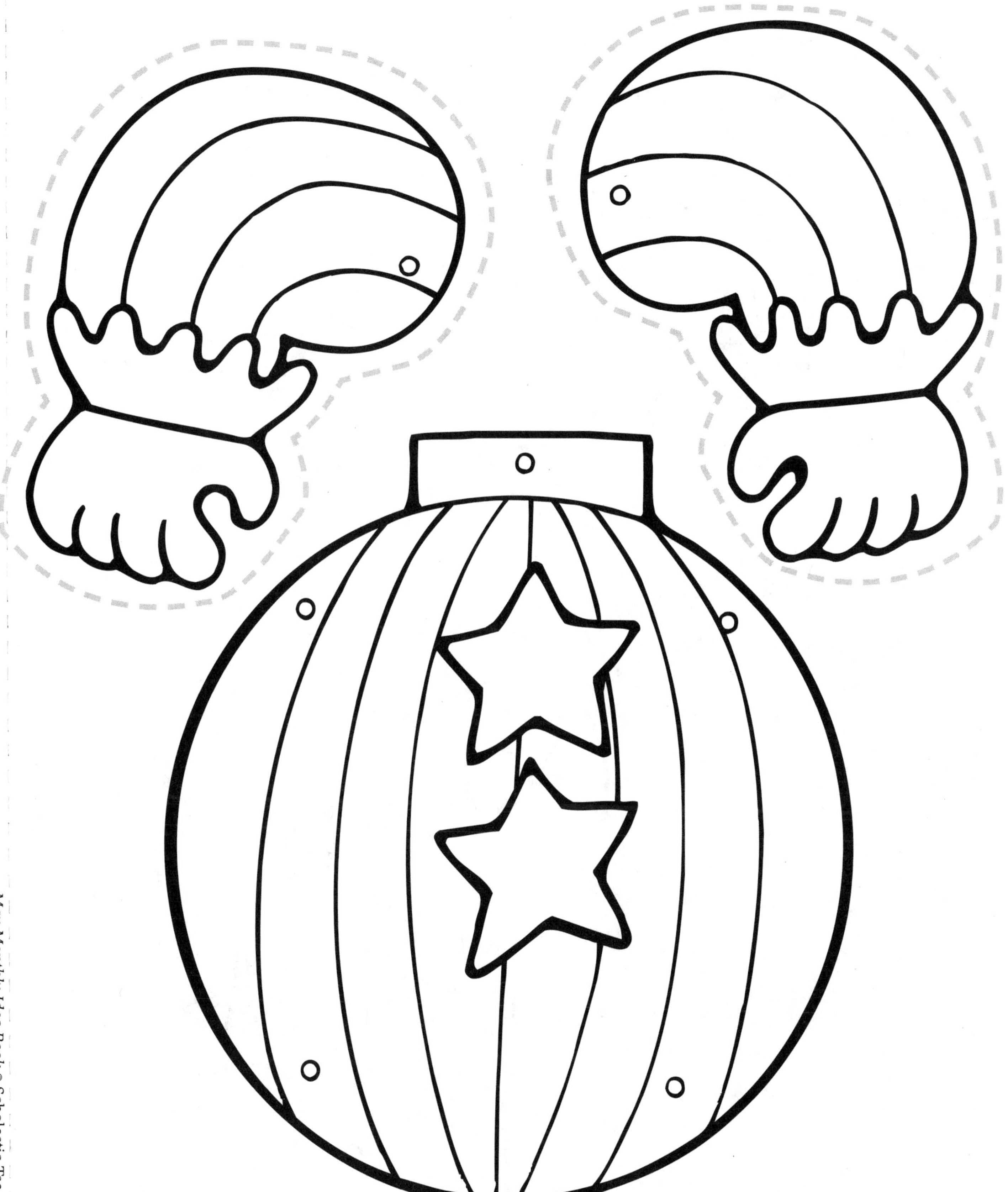

Cut out.

Cut out.

Cut out.

Cut out.

*May Monthly Idea Book* © Scholastic Teaching Resources

Cut out.  Cut out.

Cut out.  Cut out.

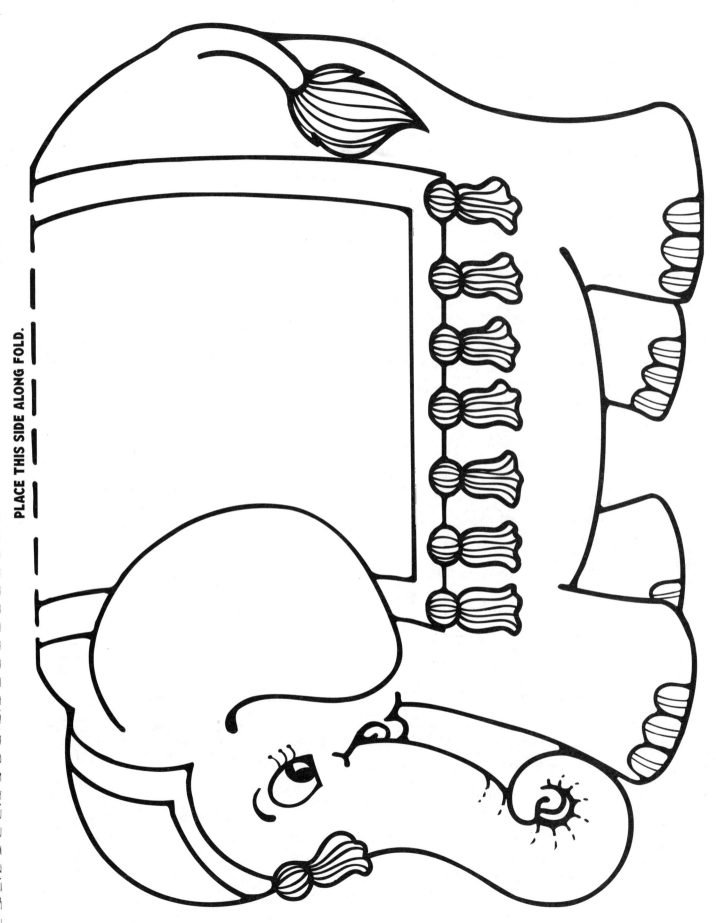

PLACE THIS SIDE ALONG FOLD.

# AWARDS, INCENTIVES, AND MORE

## Getting Started

Make several photocopies of the reproducibles on pages 138 through 142. Giving out the bookmarks, pencil toppers, notes, and certificates will show students your enthusiasm for their efforts and achievements. Plus, bookmarks and pencil toppers are a fun treat for students celebrating birthdays.

- Provide materials for decorating, including markers, color pencils, and stickers.

- Encourage students to bring home their creations to share and celebrate with family members.

### ★ BOOKMARKS

1. Photocopy onto tagboard and cut apart.

2. For more fanfare, punch a hole on one end and tie on a length of colorful ribbon or yarn.

### ★ PENCIL TOPPERS

1. Photocopy onto tagboard and cut out.

2. Use an art knife to cut through the Xs.

3. Slide a pencil through the Xs as shown.

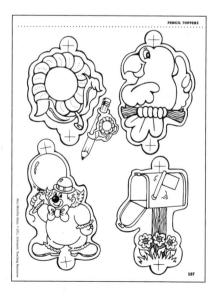

## ★ SEND-HOME NOTES

**1.** Photocopy and cut apart.

**2.** Record the child's name and the date.

**3.** Add your signature.

**4.** Add more details about the student's day on the back of the note.

## ★ CERTIFICATES

**1.** Photocopy.

**2.** Record the child's name and other information, as directed.

**3.** Add details about the child's achievement (if applicable), then add your signature and the date.

Read!

Read!

Read!

Visit the Library and....

Read

Fly

High

at the
Library!

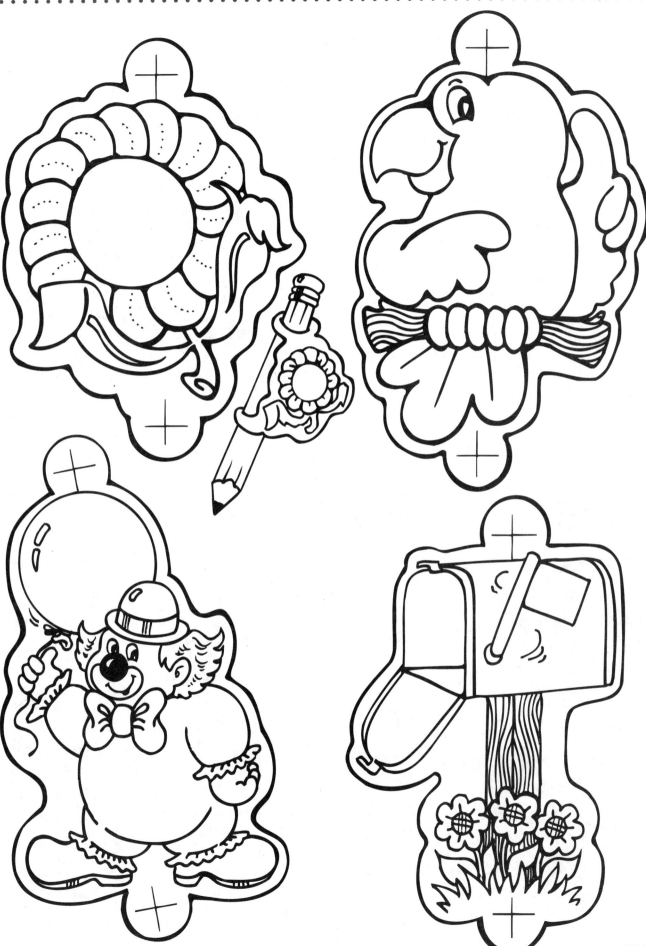

_____
Student's Name

really blossomed today!

_____     _____
Teacher                          Date

_____
Student's Name

## was a real joy today!

_____     _____
Teacher                          Date

_____
Student's Name

## was a perfect student today!

_____
Teacher

_____
Date

_____
Student's Name

## was a perfect student today!

_____
Teacher

_____
Date

# Student of the Week

Name _____

School _____

Date _____

Teacher _____

# Certificate of Recognition

**presented to**

_____
Name

**in recognition of**

_____

_____

_____

_____
Teacher

_____
Date

*May Monthly Idea Book* © Scholastic Teaching Resources

## Flower Word Find, page 30

```
G N M K L O P L K M K N E G A S W E R T X
A C W D V F M N F V K E S E D F T G H Y U
Z R I E I D A F F O D I L I N A T A B N B
Q O S D C R R C K E T Y A R C U S T O M N
A M E R A V I T Z Y Y E N S C Y H R G D J
A R N B O U G A I N V I L L E A A R T Y Y
X T C L A F O R N O I T L W E R C B F M I
Q I X U D B L F N M O S H A L R I D I R U
A L D E I H D E I B L M E S P O P P Y T E
Z L X B O G T F A R E F A P S W N B S M U
A A F E S E R A P E T H T S T M I E T C T
W O S L L J P L O R N S H D R C R S A Y N
M T D L A P S E N O R R E F G R I S W E R
A R A S T E R C V J A C R O C U S H J K L
```

## Parts-of-a-Flower Diagram, page 31

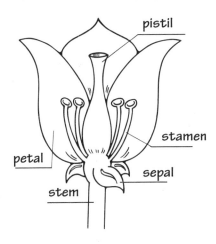

pistil
petal
stamen
sepal
stem

## Spanish Word Find, page 46

```
G Ñ M K L O P L K M K Ñ E G A S W E R T X
A S W D V F R Ñ F V K E S E D F T G H Y U
Z R I E I D S E D R A W P I Ñ A T A B Ñ B
Q T S D C R I C K E T Y A R C U S T O M Ñ
A O E R A V B T H Y Y E Ñ S C V H R G D J
A R Ñ A T C O A D S E Ñ O R I T A R T Y I
X T C O A F E R T O I T L W E C C B F M I
Q I X C D B G F D M E S A A L A I D I R U
A L D F I H X E R B Y M O S Q U E T E T E
Z L X C O G T F R R D F G P S D N B S M U
A A F F S E R A P E R H E S T I D E T C T
W O S X L J P L O R Ñ S C D R C A S A Y Ñ
M T D Ñ A P S E Ñ O R R T F G R D S W E R
A S D E R Q X C V J A Z U A T Y Ñ H J K L
```

Draw lines to match these facts about Mexico.

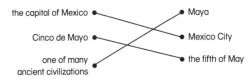

the capital of Mexico ● ● Maya
Cinco de Mayo ● ● Mexico City
one of many ancient civilizations ● ● the fifth of May

## Family Word Find, page 59

```
G N M K L O P L K M K N E G A S W E R T X
A B W N V F R N F N E I G H B O R G H Y U
F R I E N D X E D R A W P I A A T A S N B
Q O S P C R I C K E T Y G R B U S T I M N
A T E H A V B T H Y Y E R S Y V H R S D J
A H N E T C O A D S E N A R I A U N T P Y
Q R X C D B B F G R A N D M O T H E R R U
A L C F I H X E R B Y M F S Q U E T E T E
Z L O C O G T F R R D F A T H E R B S M U
A A U N C L E A P E R H T S T I D E T C T
W O S X L J P L O M O T H E R C A S A Y N
M T I N A P S E N O R R E F G R D S W E R
A S N I E C E C V J A Z R A T Y Z H J K L
```

## Bird Word Find, page 72

```
G N M K L O P M K M K P E G A G W E R T X
A S W D V F R E F V K E S E D R T G H Y U
Z R C H I C K A D E E L P I L O O N B N B
Q T A D C S I D K P T I A R Q U A I L F N
A O R G O R I O L E Y C N S C S H R G L J
A R D A T C O W D S E A O R I E A R T Y Y
X T I O A G O L D F I N C H E C T B F C I
Q I N C D B G A D M E S A A L A H D I A U
A L A F I H X R K B Y M O S Q U R T E T E
Z Y L C M O C K I N G B I R D Y A B S C U
A A F F W E R A P E R H E S T I S E T H E
W O S X R O A D R U N N E R R C H S A E N
M T P H E A S A N T R I T F G R E S W R R
A S D E N Q X C V J A Z U A T Y R H J K L
```

## Bird Diagram, page 73

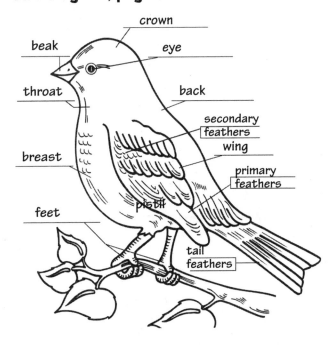

crown
beak
eye
throat
back
secondary feathers
wing
breast
primary feathers
pistil
feet
tail feathers

## Animals of Africa Word Find, page 97

```
G N M E E R K A T M K N A G C S W A R C X
A S W D V F R N F P S C N T H F T A H R U
Z Q U E I D S E D I A W T I P A T R B O J
N P A D A X I C H L U M E R M I S D O C N
A L E R N Y B T H A Y E L S E V H V X O J
F L A M I N G O D N E N O Z E B R A P D S
X A C O A L O R T A I T P W E C D R F I G
Q Y X C D B R H I N O C E R O S I K T L U
A D F Y I H I E R T Y H O S G U E T R E S
Z L X C O R L F R K D E G P S D N B S M Y
L I O N D S L P O R A E H S G I R A F F E
W O H Y E N A L O R N T C D R C A S A M N
M T D N A G T E N O R A T F P R D S W E R
A S D E M O S T R I C H U L E O P A R D L
```

## Circus Word Find, page 123

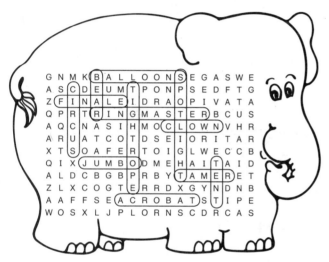

```
G N M K B A L L O O N S E G A S W E
A S C D E U M T P O N P S E D F T G
Z F I N A L E I D R A O P I V A T A
Q P R T R I N G M A S T E R B C U S
A Q C N A S I H M O C L O W N V H R
A R U A T C O T D S E I O R I T A R
X T S O A F E R T O I G L W E C C B
Q I X J U M B O D M E H A I T A I D
A L D C B G B P R B Y T A M E R E T
Z L X C O G T E R R D X G Y N D N B
A A F F S E A C R O B A T S T I P E
W O S X L J P L O R N S C D R C A S
```

**Unscramble each word. Write it on the line.**

nupetsa      peanuts

norpopc      popcorn

*May Monthly Idea Book* © Scholastic Teaching Resources